STRANGE JOURNEY

STRANGE JOURNEY

THE ILLUSTRATED ORAL HISTORY OF *THE ROCKY HORROR PICTURE SHOW*

BASED ON THE AWARD-WINNING DOCUMENTARY
STRANGE JOURNEY: THE STORY OF ROCKY HORROR

FOREWORD BY **RICHARD O'BRIEN** • INTRODUCTION BY **LINUS O'BRIEN** • EDITED BY **MALCOLM CROFT**

CONTENTS

FOREWORD

I have ruminated upon this odd little musical for over fifty years now, and I am still overwhelmed by its resilience and refusal to lie down and be ignored.

It was first performed in a tiny upstairs-studio theater (small room) at the top of the Royal Court Theatre in London's Sloane Square. In the early 1950s, the theater had been leased by an ambitious group who had called themselves the English Stage Company and had formed to encourage, stage, and promote new plays and writers.

It was a noble decision that had come about by the explosion of new theater that had arrived across the Atlantic in postwar America, where authors such as Tennessee Williams, Clifford Odets, and Arthur Miller were delivering works of both poetry and muscularity. The ESCo finally got what they thought that they had been looking for when, in 1956, John Osborne penned the first British "kitchen-sink" drama entitled *Look Back in Anger*.

Our offering was regarded as "slumming," and although enjoyed greatly by the ESCo, it became something of an embarrassment when held up against the light of their rather lofty ideals.

When the ESCo celebrated their fiftieth anniversary, it was our show that was voted by all those asked to select the one show that they would like to see resurrected upon the main stage; this was a disappointment to the ESCo, as they didn't feel that we deserved the accolade. They didn't even provide any signage for that particular event, and now, here we are. It is a wonderfully uplifting and ironic coincidence that it is our show that embodies precisely what they had been hoping for all along: a show that has had a huge effect upon its audiences all over the world and has contributed to social change in a way that they (or us) could never have imagined; it has become a very muscular piece of theater, indeed.

Here's to love and life and laughter,
Here's to happy ever after,
With the wit to spit and hit the evil eye,
Keep the rainbow banner flying high.

Richard O'Brien

DISCOVERING ROCKY

A Conversation with Trixie Mattel

I first heard about *The Rocky Horror Show* when I was seventeen years old, in the summer, a month before I went to college. I was shopping at the Shopko in Marinette, Wisconsin. And in this bargain bin—that's right, *a bargain bin*—there was a DVD with this man with high heels on the front of it and these big red lips. I was like, "It's five dollars. It looks weird. I'm gonna like it." I took it home and watched it, and my reaction was similar to those YouTube videos when someone's cochlear implant is turned on for the first time. "Oh my gosh!" I thought. "I've never tasted, seen, smelled anything like this!" When the movie ended, I watched the credits . . . and then watched it again. It was as if the radio had played a song that I had never heard before.

At that time, I was in a very primal stage of what I called "hating myself." But this film, for some reason, it spoke a language to me that I could understand. It was very gay, but I was very much allowed to like it. My mom had gone to see it in a movie theater. I know my aunt (she's a lesbian) and my grandma had seen it. Grandpa knew about it. It was a really gay thing that everyone knew about and nobody had a problem with it, so I could outwardly like it. As soon I watched it at home, I knew I needed to go see it in the movie theater. I told my mom and my aunt, "I'm going to go see *Rocky Horror* at the Oriental Theatre," and they then both told me their personal stories of having seen it in the theater when they were my age. So, *Rocky* was the beginning of an important conversation for me. I hadn't had any of "those" conversations with my family yet. I had not yet talked about my sexuality to my family. (One time, my mom found homosexual pornography on our family computer . . . and I blamed the Russians! I'm not sure if anybody believed me.) But a year after I'd seen *Rocky*, and I was halfway through my freshman year in college, I came out. I thought it was going to be dramatic, like it is on television: Your parents freak out, you cry, you run away, and you live with a man in the park. *I was hoping for something like that.* But my mom let me down. She knew. We all knew. It was so obvious.

The first time I saw *Rocky* in a theater, I was seventeen and a half years old, and I made a trip to Milwaukee with a girl from my high school. She was a conservative, rather religious, but she loved musicals. Even though I'm sure she and I to this day don't have the same politics, as teenagers, she liked musicals and I was gay as house. We went dressed as Brad and Janet. I had on the blue robe, the tighty-whities, the glasses, and the big V on my forehead. I couldn't believe she and I were at this thing together. It was so sexy and crazy and wild. People wore high heels and fishnets and were covered in glitter and fake blood, screaming.

When "Science Fiction/Double Feature" started, the lights went low, the spotlight came on, and the shadow cast began. It was like being on another planet (Janet). I didn't have the words to describe it. My understanding of myself was so small, and my understanding of the gay world was even smaller. But the *Rocky* experience was like a pop-up book: rock and roll and sex and drugs and porn . . . and the power of all of it at once. I don't remember anything about it now, though. I must have blacked out after seeing it. I remember everyone saying, "A long time ago in a galaxy far, far away" and "Let there be lips!" and I remember "Science Fiction/Double Feature" starting, but I didn't blink once from that point on. At that time, the Internet existed—I had dial-up—so I knew beforehand

that people were going to be yelling and throwing rice and all that, but I didn't really understand the ritual of it, not like I do now. I felt both brand-new and *included*.

From there, my experience with *Rocky* went zero to sixty very quickly. By the second time I watched it in a movie theater, *I was in it.* I had joined a shadow cast at the Oriental Theatre in Milwaukee, Wisconsin, with the cast of Sensual Daydreams. I knew I needed an experience such as *Rocky* to shake the shit out of me, make me less afraid of the city people after eighteen years of living in the country. I needed an environment where all of my impulses were encouraged and rewarded. At first, I was a Transylvanian in the cast, making prop bags and moving props, interacting with the audience. It was my first time seeing a drag queen too. I'm still friends with him—Harry James Hanson. He was the "Trixie" in that cast, the Usherette, who did it in drag. Seeing him was a very important beginning process of me coming out of my small-town shell, grabbing that yarn, and just starting to pull.

When I was in *Rocky*, whoever played the Usherette at the start was called the "Trixie." The Trixie would sell the survival kits—my first taste of retail. One week, I played the Trixie as a Barbie doll character, and that's when I started to figure out that it was maybe a good vibe for me. That was the first time I ever did drag, though I didn't call it drag then because most of the shadow cast was straight men and women, and they were just cross-dressing. (I performed as Janet a couple times too. She became my first safe environment to put on high heels. It was a very valuable experience to be able to do drag without calling it drag.) Ironically enough, I don't know if everybody knows this, but my stepdad, who I had a very tough relationship with, he too started calling me a "Trixie" when I was acting too feminine or too emotional. (For him, calling me a "Trixie" was akin to calling me a faggot.) Obviously, now, Trixie is the reason I've been able to travel the world and have clothes on my back. The name went from being the worst thing I could think of being called to a name given to me by my first chosen family—my *Rocky* shadow cast family. By the time I turned twenty-one, I had spent most of my teens being in *Rocky*.

For me, *The Rocky Horror Show* is timeless. Everybody understands it. I don't even think you need to be theater literate. For fifty years, the power of it and the way it's understood by the person who watches it can't really be defined. Everybody gets something different out of it, and yet *we all get the same thing out of it.* I obviously felt it down in my bones, in my cells. More than any other movie, *Rocky* has had a huge impact on me. It introduced me to an environment where I can meet other gay people and, more importantly, meet people I knew would not care that I was gay. And for that, I'll always be thankful.

Excerpted from Trixie's interview for Strange Journey*, 2024*

"I love everything about *Rocky*. I love 'The Time Warp.' I love the moment where the elevator opens and Janet faints and Frank enters. That's the moment when everyone become glued to the screen. The screen gets bigger in the moments where Frank looks at the camera—it happens a few times—and you think, 'This person is fucking with me. This person is fucking with this movie and my perception of what a film is!' It's as if the film suddenly becomes 3D. It's amazing."

—Trixie Mattel

Trixie Mattel, 2022.

INTRODUCTION

by Linus O'Brien

R*ocky Horror* has been ubiquitous in my life since I was born in 1972. At the age of four, one of my earliest memories involves attending the original stage production of *The Rocky Horror Show* at the Essoldo theater on the King's Road in London, where the technical crew let me help operate lighting during the curtain call. The original stage show was scary and not just for a four-year-old. The ushers used to wear these smoked transparent masks when they led the public to their seats while never uttering a word. Experiences such as this continued throughout my early life. I recall traveling with my father at age ten to the German Operatic Society's production in Düsseldorf and being wholly captivated while witnessing Brad and Janet hurtle out of a car through the audience while narrowly escaping a plunge into a giant pit of fire arising from the stage. I couldn't believe it, and I looked over at my dad, who had a rather bemused look on his face at this strange interpretation of his work. Over the years, I've had the opportunity to attend various anniversaries, conventions, and stage productions in the West End and on Broadway, and met inspiring and talented people from all walks of life along the way.

The endless comments left by fans who watched a video online of Tim Curry's legendary performance of the anthemic song, "I'm Going Home," were remarkably touching. One comment was from a soldier deployed in Iraq who played the song while contemplating his return home, and another from a daughter who had played it at her mother's funeral; every comment was more heartfelt than the last. These public sentiments revealed to our family, personally, the profound impact *Rocky* has had on so many lives over the past fifty years. As a result of our documentary, individuals reach out to me every day with notes expressing how much *Rocky* has positively impacted or even saved their lives:

> *I would like you to thank your dad (Richard O'Brien) for me because since watching* Rocky *my mental health has improved a lot thanks to his great work. He has helped a sixteen-year-old to want to go on living.*

My purpose in directing *Strange Journey* and producing this companion book is the hope that *Rocky Horror* will continue to touch people's lives around the world in a cathartic manner, and the enduring spirit and joy of *Rocky* will continue to foster communities globally for generations to come. Additionally, if you find it challenging to grasp some of the themes of *Rocky Horror*, consider putting yourself in the shoes of those less fortunate or struggling, and reflect on the phrase, "There, but for the grace of God, go I."

Above: Linus (left) interviewing his father for the Strange Journey *documentary.*
Opposite: Richard holding Linus, c. 1972.

CREATURES OF THE NIGHT: THE CAST

Richard O'Brien

Belinda Sinclair

Jim Sharman

Barry Bostwick

Nell Campbell

Main Cast and Crew

Tim Curry: Dr. Frank-N-Furter (a Scientist)

Richard O'Brien: Riff Raff (a Handyman) and the Show's Creator

Susan Sarandon: Janet Weiss (a Heroine) (*Picture Show*)

Barry Bostwick: Brad Majors (a Hero) (*Picture Show*)

Patricia Quinn: Magenta (a Domestic)

Nell Campbell: Columbia (a Groupie)

Peter Hinwood: Rocky Horror (a Creation) (*Picture Show*)

Meat Loaf: Eddie (a Delivery Boy)**

Belinda Sinclair: Janet (a Heroine) (*Stage Show*)

Rayner Bourton: *Rocky Horror* (a Creation) (*Stage Show*)**

Jim Sharman (a Director)

Richard Hartley (a Musical Director)

Sue Blane (a Costume Designer)

Brian Thomson (a Set Designer)**

Joel Thurm (a Casting Director)

John Goldstone (a Producer)

Lou Adler (a Producer)

Susan Sarandon

Lou Adler

Friends and Fans

Jack Black (a Rock Star)

Tim Deegan (a Hero)**

Dori Hartley (a Frank)**

Trixie Mattel (a Friend)

Chrissie Shrimpton Messenger (a Friend)

Karen Tongson (a Professor)

Lillias Piro (a *Rocky Horror* Elder)

Sal Piro (a *Rocky Horror* Founding Elder)**

Tristan Ratterman (a Shadow Cast Performer)

Sean Waters (a Shadow Cast Performer)

Jeffrey Weinstock (a Professor)

(Editor's note: All entries in this book are excerpted from interviews conducted by Linus O'Brien for the documentary *Strange Journey*, except where noted with an ** above; these excerpts were obtained from archival interviews.)

Tim Curry

Patricia Quinn

Sue Blane

Richard Hartley

CHAPTER 1

IT WAS GREAT WHEN IT ALL BEGAN

As blood-red lips emerge from the void ready to sing, it's time for the celebration of *The Rocky Horror Show* to begin. This musical's journey to immortality has been a strange one, starting when it was nothing more than a naughty little twinkle in Richard O'Brien's eyes. If you're ready, then . . . let there be lips . . .

From top left: Older brother Bob; grandfather and grandmother; sister Gillian. Seated in front: Richard (left) and brother Robin.

The story of Rocky Horror *begins not in London but in New Zealand with a directionless hairdresser looking for something new. How new, the world was yet to find out. We start at the very beginning with our protagonist, Rocky's creator, Richard O'Brien.*

Richard O'Brien I nearly died at birth. I wasn't supposed to last the night. But I did. I was the youngest of four children and came from a tough background. My father was an accountant. But I was always a dreamer. I was always one of those kids that loved dressing up and performing. I wanted to live in a world of make-believe. Whether that had anything to do with my transgendered nature, as well, I've got no idea. I would imagine so.

My parents immigrated to New Zealand in 1952 when I was ten,and I went through pubescence and adolescence there. I was lucky to live right next door to the theater. They mostly showed films, especially late-night movies, and the manager would give me posters and first-run sheets. I even had *Rebel Without a Cause*—no idea what that would be worth now. I just stuck them under my bed. But they fueled my obsession for the movies.

I used to go to see B-movies and science-fiction films at the Embassy cinema in Hamilton, New Zealand, on Friday and Saturday nights. They'd usually have a double feature, starting around 11 p.m. I was just a boy, maybe sixteen or seventeen, with nowhere else to be, so I'd go and watch whatever was playing, even if it was late.

In 1964, at the age of twenty-two, I'd been cutting hair for five years, but I didn't want to do that for the rest of my life. I didn't actually know what I wanted to do. I was directionless. So I got on a boat, the *Castel Felice*, an Italian shipping liner. For £112, I spent five weeks at sea traveling from Auckland up to Singapore, from Singapore to the Red Sea, through the Suez Canal, to Bombay before Naples . . . and then England.

Jim Sharman In the late '60s, I was an independent theater director, though I had gotten an early start by directing Mozart's *Don Giovanni* when I was twenty-one—which caused a bit of a scandal. Then I directed *Hair* in Australia. Before leaving Australia, and prior to working on *Jesus Christ Superstar*, I made a very short, very inexpensive

Richard (left) in his rockabilly phase, with friends.

"I've never wanted fame, I've never wanted to be famous, and I've never wanted to be rich. My WHEN IT ALL BEGAN motto has always been 'The greatest thing you'll ever learn is just to love and be loved in return.' That's success."

—Richard O'Brien

Above: Jim Sharman directing Jesus Christ Superstar. *Below: Richard in a photo booth, c. 1970.*

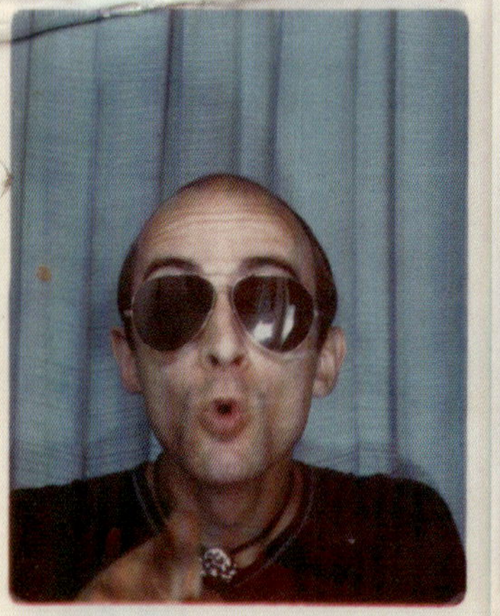
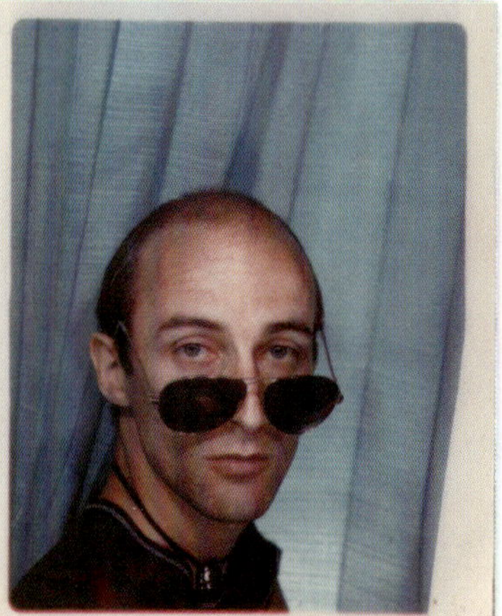

underground film called *Shirley Thompson vs. the Aliens*. It was a mix of rock and roll, science fiction, and psychological drama. Then I directed *Superstar* in Australia, which caught the attention of its lyricist, Tim Rice, and the producer, Robert Stigwood. They asked me to direct *Superstar* in London's West End. When it opened, it received particularly favorable reviews—which hadn't always been the case with my early productions.

Richard O'Brien In 1965, I went to drama school to learn how to act. I did wonder then whether you can be taught to act? I'm not quite sure. I think probably what you need to be taught is how to not act. Reacting is what makes the best actors. At that time, acting was the important thing in my life. I didn't want to be a celebrity. I just wanted to play make-believe.

Chrissie Messenger (Shrimpton) The first time I met Richard, we were both at a rather shabby drama school called the Actors Workshop in London in the mid-1960s, a poor imitation of the one in New York. We became very close friends very quickly. He had this deep, sensitive quality that not a lot of people had back then.

Richard O'Brien My friend Chrissie Shrimpton—Mick Jagger's then-girlfriend, and sister of model Jean Shrimpton—introduced me to the rockocracy. England was swinging like a pendulum. There was nowhere better to be on the planet. My first jazz cigarette was at drama school in 1965 with Chrissie. One day I got a phone call, and it was Chrissie and she said, "I've got some of that stuff that you thought you might like to test if you want to come around tonight." And so I went around to Mick Jagger's apartment. In the living room, she skinned up. I've never looked back!

Chrissie Messenger (Shrimpton) In the early days, I was living quite the high life while Richard was sharing a room with a flatmate. We had very different lives. Richard was like the poor, starving artist. Although he wanted to ask me to marry him, we never had a romantic relationship. We had a romantic friendship.

Richard O'Brien By '67–'68, I'd finished drama school and was writing songs. Chrissie was auditioning at the Mermaid Theatre for *Gulliver's Travels*, and she invited me along. She didn't get the part, but I did. The director, Sean Kenny, took a liking to me and often invited me to restaurants and introduced me to people such as Andrew Loog Oldham, the Rolling Stones' then-manager. I didn't know why, but influential people kept taking me under their wing. Maybe they saw some talent in me—I don't know—but I felt lucky.

Around this time, I walked into Decca Records on London's South Bank with a guitar. I said, "I've come to sing some songs." The receptionist asked if I had an appointment, and I said, "No, but you're a record company, and I'm a singer-songwriter." I wasn't completely lying. She hesitated, but then a man named Dick Rowe, who had turned down the Beatles, came over. He said, "It doesn't

Left: Chrissie Shrimpton with then-boyfriend Mick Jagger. Right: Richard and Chrissie.

Above: Richard O'Brien (right) during the tour of Hair. *Paul Nicholas, who starred as Berger, is second from left. Opposite: A young Richard O'Brien with a guitar.*

"Chrissie introduced me to the rockocracy. England was swinging like a pendulum. There was nowhere better to be on the planet."

—Richard O'Brien

work like that, but come to my office." He sent me to a music publisher in Soho Square.

Nell Campbell In 1971, I left Sydney for London, having turned eighteen just two weeks earlier. I took on all sorts of hilarious jobs when I arrived. I worked in Kensington Market, where a guy called Freddie on a stall across from me would always talk about a singer in a band. We'd drink cups of tea and eat cheap jam donuts. His band, Queen, eventually got signed. I also spent a lot of time busking. I'd dress in top hat and tails.

Richard O'Brien In 1969, there was a *Hair* tour, and I joined, traveling the country. That's where I met Kimi [Wong], my first wife, and mother to my son, Linus. After the tour, I returned to London and joined *Hair* in the West End. Around that time, *Jesus Christ Superstar* was being cast, and everyone in *Hair* auditioned—it was an exciting time.

Belinda Sinclair I first met Richard O'Brien during *Hair*. I thought, "What a crazy dude." But we were all crazy back then, so he wasn't particularly unusual.

Tim Curry When I was in *Hair*, we used to socialize with the touring company. Richard O'Brien and Kimi, Richard's wife, were in the touring company. That's how I first knew of Richard.

Belinda Sinclair One night after the show [of *Hair*], a lot of us went back to Richard's house. The TV was on, and I think an old B-movie was playing. Richard had his acoustic guitar, strumming away as he always did in between preparing drinks. He

How I Love Those "B" Movies.

In the 50's, low budget films were in a class of their own. Just how many were made is inestimable – some were dreadful some were excellent – but most of them had one thing in common – the "style" of their acting.

If you remember going to the pictures as a kid – then, later, in somebody's garden or on a vacant lot or somewhere you and your friends would re-live the movie (if you were lucky, you got the Cornel Wilde part) then the "B movie style" will be no stranger to you. The B movie style is made up of several ingredients – Direct action

Bad casting

Black and white values

Comic strip dialogue

and

One hundred per cent belief

Sci fi

The last quality being all important. Imagine a film being made in the early 50's with a hero and heroine, scientist and an opposing force, say an alien monster. (The monster would take of itself) But the three lead actors all of whom are not and never will be big household names are suddenly thrust into a four to (if lucky) six weeks world of make believe – there is no time for character analysis no time for subtlety and so they play it – the hero looking like a cross between a truck driver and a football player the heroine supporting his (the hero's) masculinity and the scientist who would look more at home slicing salt beef in a kosher Brooklyn sandwich bar.

It's banality time but played for real (no pastiche) they know they're not who they pretend to be and you know it as well – but when the scientist picks a piece of metal and says that ("quite frankly its molecular structure is beyond the realms of my scientific knowledge; it's probably part of some alien space craft.") believe it or not it's a great moment.

~~When the heroine in "The Creature from the Black Lagoon" asks the hero what it was like in the lagoon~~

IN "THE CREATURE FROM THE BLACK LAGOON" THE HEROINE ASKS THE HERO WHO HAS JUST RETURNED FROM A SKINDIVING EXPEDITION IN THE LAGOON, "WHAT WAS IT LIKE DOWN THERE?" HE ANSWERS.

"IT WAS LIKE ANOTHER WORLD" BUT IT'S DELIVERED AS THOUGH IT IS THE SECRETS OF THE COSMOS. — So, WHAT WAS INITIALLY THE STAMP OF A SECOND RATE MOVIE IS NOW A STYLE - A STYLE THAT THE THEATRE HAS NOW ADDED TO IT'S REPETOIRE — ELIZABETHAN, JACOBEAN, RESTORATION, MELLODRAMA, HIGH CAMP, KITCHEN SINK AND NOW "B MOVIE". I LOVE IT, BRODERICK CRAWFORD MOVE OVER.

Previous pages: An early writing by Richard on his love for B-movies lays the groundwork for Rocky Horror.
Opposite: Richard O'Brien with Linus in a park, debating moving back to New Zealand.

said something like, "I'm going to write my own musical, and wouldn't it be great if the story was like a B-movie and the music was rock and roll?" We all went, "Yeah, yeah, great idea!" And that was it. He started writing it right there.

Jeffrey Weinstock The early-'70s theater scene was all about pushing boundaries: *Hair* promoted a free-love philosophy, *Jesus Christ Superstar* took an iconoclastic approach to divinity, and *Rocky Horror* took both even further with its themes of transvestitism and bisexuality.

Jim Sharman After *Jesus Christ Superstar* opened in London, I wanted to return to my independent, experimental theater roots. I had connections at the Royal Court Theatre. That's when I was introduced to Nicky Wright and Harriet Cruickshank, who were managing the Royal Court's Theatre Upstairs. They told me, "If you find a play, let us know."

In late 1972, Richard's life changed beyond all recognition, somewhat ironically for an atheist, with the arrival of Jesus Christ Superstar, *a second coming that offered Richard his first opportunity to be a superstar in his own right. Well, sort of.*

Richard O'Brien In the early 1970s, Britain had open auditions for new shows—two or three days where anyone could get five or ten minutes onstage. It was a bit of a cattle call, but who cared? I landed a role in *Jesus Christ Superstar* and was set to take over as King Herod after an American actor, Paul Jabara's, three-month Equity waiver expired.

Jim Sharman I first came across Richard O'Brien during *Jesus Christ Superstar*, and I was immediately struck by his look. He has a very gaunt but striking appearance—there was a touch of Max Schreck from Nosferatu about him.

Richard O'Brien I had only one line in *Jesus Christ Superstar.* "See my purse, I'm a poor poor man." I used to sing it with great gusto onstage. The director wanted me to play Herod like a rock and roll star. I was more than delighted with the idea. Elvis Presley was my idol. I had this wonderful white suit with gold lapels and did this great rock and roll dance. After just two practices, they threw me into a Friday matinee to see how I would do. Robert Stigwood, the producer, sat in the box and, like Caesar, gave me a thumbs-down after the show. They brought someone else in, which breached my contract. They paid me £300 and sent me home. In hindsight, it was the best thing that ever happened to me. If I had taken over the role of Herod, I wouldn't have written *Rocky Horror*. In a way, I wrote *Rocky Horror* out of spite.

Chrissie Messenger Richard was devastated to be fired from *Jesus Christ Superstar*. Absolutely devastated. You couldn't help but feel devastated for him. He was not only out of the show, but he was also outraged. It was a dreadful time for him. But, if he hadn't been fired, *Rocky Horror* would never have been made.

Richard O'Brien Jim, the director of *Superstar*, pulled me aside before I left. He apologized, saying he hadn't known it would happen. I assumed it was just lip service, but then he said, "I think you have talent, and I'd like to work with you again." I thanked him, not thinking much of it at the time. It was very nice for me to leave the theater with that in my ear, but I didn't truly believe him.

As a new parent, I felt the pressure to stay employed. I debated whether to return to New Zealand for a "proper" job or continue acting. Then someone asked me to entertain the EMI film studio crew for their Christmas party. I wrote some jokes and a song about my favorite movies—"Science Fiction/Double Feature." That night, I did my fifteen-minute set and got the crew laughing. The applause and laughter was overwhelming. That was it—the moment that changed my life. I decided to stick with writing songs a little longer. In the New Year of 1973, I wondered whether it might serve as prologue to the germ of an idea that I had for a musical.

"I first met Richard O'Brien during *Hair*. I thought, 'What a crazy dude.' But we were all crazy back then, so he wasn't particularly unusual."

—Belinda Sinclair

Richard Hartley c. 1972.

Richard's brief stint as a superstar may have been over, but not his association with Jim Sharman. The Royal Court's Theatre Upstairs and The Unseen Hand *would open even more doors.*

Jim Sharman Through some connections, I met Sam Shepard. I told him about my experiences making my first movie, *Shirley Thompson vs. the Aliens*, in Australia, and in turn, he told me about his play *The Unseen Hand*. That became one of three productions I staged at the Royal Court with set designer Brian Thomson, who had traveled with me to London from Australia. These productions—what would now be called immersive theater—were staged in the Theatre Upstairs.

Richard O'Brien Not long after I was let go from *Superstar*, Jim Sharman called and invited me to the Royal Court Theatre. He was directing *The Unseen Hand* by Sam Shepard and wanted me in it. We played in the upstairs fringe space, and it completely sold out. It was a small production but a big success. That's when I met Richard Hartley, our musical director. We connected instantly—both war babies, both from working-class backgrounds, both shaped by the same music.

Richard Hartley I was in a rock and roll band in the '60s. After that, I started arranging music for bands on television. They'd have an artist on the show, and I'd do the arrangement. I knew a musical director who was working on *Jesus Christ Superstar* in the West End. He said to me, "You understand

Warren Clark (left) as Blue Morphan and Richard O'Brien as Willie in The Unseen Hand.

these pop voices, don't you?" So, I went to the auditions, and that's where I met Jim Sharman. Later, Jim called me about writing some music for a Sam Shepard play, *The Unseen Hand*. He wanted something quite avant-garde. That's how I connected with Richard O'Brien. I thought Richard was very skinny when I first met him. He had long, straggly hair—he had hair in those days—and was very energetic.

Richard O'Brien *The Unseen Hand* wasn't meant to be a comedy, but our version became one—largely because of me. Sam was fine with it and even wrote me a final line. I played Willie the Space Freak, switching between a Peter Lorre–like voice and a Superman-style delivery. Since I'd turned the role comedic, Sam added a new ending. A cowboy says, "Hey, Willie, what are we going to do without you?" I turn, shrug, and say, "Tough bananas." That was my exit.

Hair, Jesus Christ Superstar, *and* The Unseen Hand *had brought together the main creators of* Rocky *to a strange and bewitching place: the Royal Court's Theatre Upstairs. It was here that Richard had an idea for a musical that would change his life forever. He started writing a rock and roll homage to sci-fi movies called* They Came from Denton High.

Following pages: Richard's original notes on characters and scene breakdowns, and dialogue and lyric fragments.

CAROL HAYMAN

PETER CROUCH.

CHARACTERS :- NARRATOR. - (SCHOLARLY)

BRAD MAJORS. (ALL AMERICAN BOY) (LATE 50's)

JANET WEISS. (ALL AMERICAN GIRL) " "

FRANK N. FURTER. (ALICE COOPER TYPE FRANKENSTEIN)

NAME RIFF KAFF ? (MINION) (JOE COCKER PLUS)

NAME Rocky HORRIFIC ? (BEAUTIFUL MONSTER) (ADRIAN STREET ?)

DR EVRETT SCOTT. (FRIEND AND EX-TUTOR of BRAD)

COLUMBIA

ACT 1.

SCENES :-

(1) "BRAD" & "JANET" IN CAR
EXPLAIN RELATIONSHIP, REASON FOR TRAVELING, --
PUNCTURE.

(2)
FRONTDOOR of HOUSE ON THE HILL, MEET "JOE VITUS"
ENTER IN TO HALL.

(3) ENTRANCE of "FRANK. N. FURTER"

(4) LABOROTORY AND MEETING of "Rock HORROAR."

ACT. 2.

(1) "JANET" & "FRANK . N . FURTER" (IMPERSONATING BRAD)
JANETS ROOM.

(2) BRAD & FRANK IN FRANKS ROOM. (ROCK BREAKS OUT)

(3) LABOROTORY

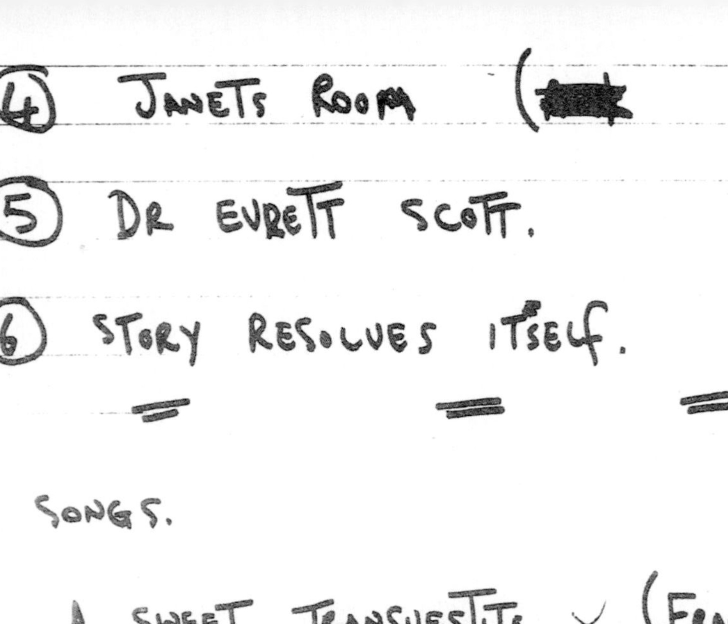

4. JANETS ROOM (

5. DR EVRETT SCOTT.

6. STORY RESOLVES ITSELF.

= = =

SONGS.

A SWEET TRANSVESTITE. ✓ (FRANK N. FURTER)
THERES A LIGHT. (FRANK - BRAD AND C°) ✓
TRIBUTE TO CHARLES ATLAS (ROCKY) & FRANK? ✓
ONCE IN A WHILE (JOE)
~~[illegible] JANET [illegible] ([illegible])~~
SWORD OF DAMOCLES - (ROCKY) ✓
WISE UP JANET WEISS (BRAD) AND ALL.
SUPER HEROES

=

(~~[illegible]~~ ~~[illegible]~~ ~~[illegible]~~)

FRANK. — HELLO — WE HAVE A VISITOR

BRAD. ~~GREAT~~ SCOTT — SCOTTY — DR EVRETT SCOTT

~~J.V.~~ RRaf YOU KNOW THIS EARTHL— — . PERSON?

BRAD — YES, I DO HE'S AN OLD FRIEND
OF MINE.

FRANK — I SEE — SO THIS WASN'T
SIMPLY A CHANCE MEETING —
YOU CAME HERE WITH A PURPOSE

BRAD — THATS NOT TRUE — MY CAR BROKE
DOWN — I TOLD YOU

FRANK — I KNOW WHAT YOU TOLD ME
BRAD — BUT THIS DR EVRETT SCOTT
HIS NAME IS NOT UNKNOWN TO ME.

BRAD — HE WAS A SCIENCE TEACHER AT
DENTON HIGH.

FRANK — AND HE NOW WORKS FOR YOUR
GOVERNMENT — DOESN'T HE BRAD?
HE'S ATTACHED TO THE BEAREUX OF THE
INVESTIGATION OF THAT WHICH YOU
CALL U.F.O'S — THATS RIGHT ISN'T
IT BRAD.

BRAD — HE MIGHT BE — I DONT KNOW.

~~J.V.~~ Raff — THE INTRUDER IS ENTERING THE
BUILDING MASTER.

FRANK AH HE'S IN THE ZEN ROOM

SEAL OFF ALL EXITS —
AND ALL DOORS — EXCEPT FOR THOSE
THAT LEAD HERE — AND I THINK
THERES TIME FOR SOME QUICK MIND
EXPANSION BEFORE HE GETS HERE.

((HE PUTS ON HEADWEAR WITH ELECTRODES))
~~[illegible]~~.)

I HOPE THERES ENOUGH ACID IN THE
BATTERIES — AH YES — (BANG)
OH MY GOD I THINK I'VE O-D'd

Riff Raff ~~J.V.~~ — MASTER — OUR VISITOR IS ALMOST
WITH US —

FRANK — WHO — OH YES — BRING RICKY AND
JANET HERE — I THINK WE SHOULD
~~[illegible]~~ MAKE THIS A SOCIAL OCCASION
THE ~~[illegible]~~ THREE UNEXPECTED GUESTS
~~[illegible]~~ SHALL ~~[illegible]~~ ENTERTAIN US WITH A
FLOOR SHOW — WHICH I SHALL DIRECT.

DOORS OPEN.

BRAD — DR SCOTT!

SCOTTY — BRAD — WHAT ARE YOU DOING HERE

FRANK — DONT PLAY GAMES DR SCOTT.
YOU KNOW FULL WELL WHAT BRAD
MAJORS IS HERE FOR — IT WAS
PART OF YOUR PLAN THAT HE
AND HIS FEMALE SHOULD CHECK

THE LAYOUT FOR YOU – UNFORTUNEATLY FOR YOU ALL – ~~I HAVE PLANS FOR YOU THAT WILL MEAN A CHANGE~~ THERE IS TO BE A CHANGE OF PLANS — I'M SURE YOU'RE ADAPTABLE DR SCOTT — I KNOW BRAD IS

DOORS OPEN.

JANET – DR SCOTT!

SCOTTY – JANET!

FRANK – RICKY!

RICKY – PISS OFF.

FRANK – LISTEN – I MADE YOU AND I CAN BREAK YOU JUST AS EASILY. I'LL PULL YOUR PLUG OUT

OK. ITS STARTIME

J.V.! — SET THE SONIC TRANSDUCER ON PROGRAMME 8 – SECURE ALL LEVELS AT ZERO –

SCOTTY – ~~YOU FIEND – YOU INTEND TO SAP OUR WILL POWER – WELL YOU'LL NOT FIND EARTH PEOPLE QUITE THE SOFT MARK YOU THINK THEY ARE~~

BRAD — YOU MEAN - - -

SCOTTY. — YES — OUR AMIABLE HOST IS AN ALIEN AN EXRATERRESTIAL BEING FROM THE PLANET OF TRAN-ZELL

BRAD — AN ALIEN

JANET — AN ALIEN. I THOUGHT IT SEEMED STRANGE

FRANK — I'D PREFER "DIFFERENT"

BRAD — YOU MEAN THAT YOU'VE - - -

JANET — NO — I MEAN THAT WE'VE - - -

BRAD — NOW LISTEN JANET

SCOTTY – You won't find Earth people quite the easy mark that you imagine – this Sonic Transducer! It is I suppose some type of audio vibratory physio molecular transport devise?

FRANK – You'd better believe it

BRAD – You mean – – – ?

SCOTTY – Yes Brad – it's something we ourselves have been working on. But it seems our friend here. Found a way of perfecting it – a devise that is capable of breaking down solid matter and then projecting it through space. And who knows, perhaps even time itself

JANET – You're going to send us to another planet?

FRANK – Planet – Shmanet Janet

~~I'll~~ TELL YOU ONCE
WONT TELL YOU TWICE
YOU'D BETTER WISE UP JANET WEISS

Y'APPLE PIE
DONT TASTE TO NICE
YOU'D BETTER WISE JANET WEISS

I'VE LAID THE SEED
IT SHOULD BE ALL YOU NEED
YOU'RE AS SENSUAL
AS A PENCIL
WOUND UP LIKE AN 'E' OR FIRST STRING
WHEN WE MADE IT ~~DID YOU HEAR A~~
D~~ID~~ ~~YA~~ HEAR A BELL RING?

Y~~ou~~' GOT A BLOCK?
TAKE MY ADVICE
YOU'D BETTER WISE UP JANET WEISS

THE TRANSDUCER
WILL SEDUCE YAH
ITS SOMETHING YOU'LL GET USED TO
A MENTAL MIND-FUCK CAN BE NICE.

YOU'D BETTER WISE UP - JANET WEISS
YOU'D BETTER WISE UP
BUILD YOUR THIGHS UP

YOU'D BETTER WISE UP

NARRATOR - AND THEN SHE CRIES OUT.

JANET — STOP!!

FRANK — DONT GET HOT AND FLUSTERED
USE A BIT OF MUSTARD.

ALL — * YOU'RE A HOT DOG
BUT YOU'D BETTER NOT TRY TO HURT HER
FRANK FURTER

*(THIS KEEPS REPEATING AND ONE BY ONE
THE THREE ENTER THE TRANSDUCER)
THEY DISSAPEAR

FRANK — COLUMBIA — THE ARTISTES ARE IN A
MOLECULAR STATE SOMEWHERE BETWEEN
US ~~YOU~~ AND ~~US~~ YOURSELF. WHEN THEY'VE
PULLED THEMSELVES TOGETHER — SEE THAT
THEY ARE PREPARED FOR THE FLOORSHOW.

COLUMBIA — (ON MONITOR) OH WOW — I CAN DIG IT —
TOO MUCH — FAR OUT — WHAT A GAS — THATS GROOVY —
IM HIP MAN — IT'S LIKE A TRIP — OH NICE ONE
FREAK OUT BABY — DIG YOU LATER.

FRANK — ~~SHE'S FLIPPED IT~~ WOW HEY MAN SHES PRETTY FAR OUT — MAN

~~(SCENE CHANGE) IN THE CAGE.~~

~~[illegible]~~

~~[illegible] WELL IT SEEMS THAT WE'VE ARRIVED~~
~~LET'S SEE IF WE CAN GET OUT OF HERE~~

SCENE CHANGE

MESSENGER ARRIVES SAYS
MISSING PERSONS HAVE COME UP
WITH WHAT MIGHT BE A LINK.

DR GOES TO GLASTONBURY TOR.

A. YOUTH HAS REPORTED HIS FRIEND MISSING
LEFT IT LATE BECAUSE HE THOUGHT
HE WAS LOONING. —
DR. GOES TO MISSING MANS ROOM.
FINDS MAP ~~[illegible]~~ OF ENGLAND WITH SEVERAL
SPOTS MARKED AND LINKED WITH RULED LINES
THEY FORM A VEE SHAPE – WITH THE WATLINGTON
FIELD AT THE APEX (>×). FRIEND OF
MISSING BOY SAYS THAT HIS FRIEND WAS A
BIT OF A HIPPIE AND SAID THAT HIPPIE HAD
CLAIMED TO HAVE SPOKEN TO EITHER SPIRITS —
ALIENS OR BEING FROM ANOTHER DIMENSION,
BUT HE THOUGHT HE WAS STONED.

FRANK. (SCREAMING)
MY MY MY MY.

IM A WILD AND UNTAMED THING
IM A BEE WITH A DEADLY STING
GET A HIT AND YOUR MIND GOES PING

COLUMBIA
MICHAEL RENNIE WAS ILL
THE DAY THE EARTH STOOD STILL
BUT HE TOLD US WHERE WE STAND
AND FLASH GORDON WAS THERE
IN SILVER UNDERWEAR
CLAUDE RAINS WAS THE INVISIBLE MAN
THEN SOMETHING WENT WRONG
FOR FAY WRAY AND KING KONG
THEY GOT CAUGHT IN A CELLULOID JAM
THEN AT A DEADLY PACE
IT CAME FROM OUTER SPACE
AND THIS IS HOW THE MESSAGE RAN.
SCIENCE FICTION – DOUBLE FEATURE
DR X WILL BUILD A CREATURE
SEE ANDROIDS FIGHTING BRAD & JANET
ANNE FRANCIS STARS IN FORBIDDEN PLANET
OH – AT THE LATE NIGHT DOUBLE FEATURE
PICTURE SHOW.
I KNEW LEO G. CARROL
WAS OVER A BARREL
WHEN TARRANTULA TOOK TO THE HILLS
AND I GOT REALLY HOT
WHEN I SAW JEANNETTE SCOTT
FIGHT A TRIFFID THAT SPITS POISON AND KILLS
AND WHEN WORLDS COLLIDE
SAID GEORGE PAL TO HIS BRIDE
I'M GOING TO GIVE YOU SOME TERRIBLE THRILLS
DANA ANDREWS SAID PRUNES
GAVE HIM THE RUNES
AND PASSING THEM USED LOTS OF SK
LET'S DO, THE.....
TIME WARP
BASIC STEPS
3.4.5.
L
R
1
L R
START
3.4.5.
R
2
1 (ITS JUST A) JUMP TO THE LEFT, WITH HANDS UP
2 A STEP TO THE RIGHT (TIME-WARPER ANNETTE FUNICELLO SUGGESTS A VERY WIDE STEP.)
3* (WITH YOUR HANDS ON YOUR HIPS)
YOU BRING YOUR KNEES IN TIGHT.
4 (THEN) THE PELVIC THRUST (IF REPEATED FIVE TIMES, IT NEARLY DRIVES YOU INSA-A-ANE)
5 HIPSWIVEL (IF NOT DRIVEN INSA-A-ANE BY STEP FOUR)
6 LET'S DO THE TIME WARP AGAIN!!
* THOSE WITH LIMB DISABILITIES MAY FIND IT NECESSARY TO ALTER OR DELETE THIS ACTION, BUT NO EXCUSES FOR ALTERATIONS TO STEPS FOUR AND FIVE.
AS FEATURED IN 'THE ROCK

Jim Sharman One day, Richard mentioned to me that he had an idea for a musical. I said, "I hope it's not religious." And of course it's the only one that ended up with its own cult.

Richard Hartley When Richard mentioned he had an idea for a rock musical, my first reaction was, "Oh my God, not another one." At that time, everyone had a rock musical in their back pocket.

Richard O'Brien I told Jim Sharman, "I'm writing a little musical. It's amusing me—maybe it'll amuse you too." Jim agreed to listen, bringing along a very reluctant Richard Hartley to our flat on Oakington Road. That night, I played "Science Fiction/Double Feature," "Over at the Frankenstein Place," and "The Sword of Damocles" and read parts of the script. Jim left without much reaction. Then—silence for three or four days. Jim finally called and said, "They want me to do another play downstairs at the Royal Court, but I told them I'll only do it if I get three weeks of fun upstairs first. So we're on." Then came the kicker: "I need twenty more pages and five new songs in two days." And just like that, we went into rehearsals.

Richard Hartley I went to Richard's flat one night early in 1973—quite late in the evening—and Jim told Richard, "Don't describe it . . . just play some songs." That's when Richard sang "Science Fiction/Double Feature" to me for the first time. It was such a beautiful song—romantic, nostalgic, all about watching movies as a kid. It was autobiographical, for sure. That was the song that really stuck with me. Jim then told Richard that he wanted to do something completely opposite of *Jesus Christ Superstar,* and he couldn't find anything more opposite than *Rocky*. It seemed like the perfect match.

Jim Sharman At Richard's house, "Science Fiction/Double Feature" convinced me to direct it. It was pretty rough at that stage, and a lot of people raised their eyebrows at the idea of me going from something as polished as *Jesus Christ Superstar* to something as raw as *They Came from Denton High*—as *Rocky* was called then. I was never interested in conventional musicals. I wanted to bring rock and roll into musicals and do away with the old show-tune style. That was exactly what drew me to Richard's play—it was a rock and roll musical.

Richard Hartley Jim was very happy when he first heard Richard's songs. He wanted to do something on the fringe. And they were definitely on the fringe.

Jim Sharman At the earliest stages, the key people I invited into the creation of *Rocky Horror* were Brian Thomson, costume designer Sue Blane—who came from Glasgow Citizens Theatre via Royal Court manager Harriet Gooch [Cruikshank]—and Richard Hartley, who had been the rehearsal pianist on *Superstar*. We were all products of a culture where late-night movies were an education. I think the fact that we were all on the same page helped create something quite unique. Sue Blane brought a much-needed sensibility from the Glasgow Citizens Theatre, which at the time was a hub for drag and avant-garde design.

Sue Blane I moved down to London from Glasgow in 1973 and was just finding my feet when I got a call from Harriet Cruickshank, who was managing the Theatre Upstairs at the Royal Court. She said, "Could you meet with a director who's been really difficult about finding someone to do the costumes for a show?" I said yes. My first vision of Jim Sharman was a pair of flared denim jeans and black-and-white platform boots with a two-inch platform!

Jim Sharman At the time, money wasn't really a challenge because we didn't have any. It was a small space and a hugely ambitious idea. Once Brian came up with the haunted cinema concept, I wanted something that would engage the audience's imagination. You never saw a car, but someone would mimic a car—and that was enough. That sense of playful invention was there throughout. The show wasn't set anywhere. The entire theater was the stage.

Above: Glam rock supergroup Sweet. Opposite: Set designer Brian Thomson, c. 1973.

Sue Blane It was the spring of '73 when Jim and I hit it off immediately. He took me out to lunch at a restaurant called Smalls, and I thought, "This is great!" I was relatively inexperienced at the time, and I had never been taken out to lunch by a director before. After that, we went to see what I think was the last night of *The Unseen Hand* at the Theatre Upstairs. Afterward, we all went to a Greek restaurant in Camden Town and got completely drunk. By three o'clock in the morning, and with the start of a terrible hangover, I was designing my *Rocky Horror* costumes. Jim never actually said, "Would you do it?" and I never said, "Yes, I'd love to." It just kind of happened.

Nell Campbell The creative, symbiotic relationship of the team was thrilling to watch. You had Jim Sharman, a talented director, especially for musicals, which are the hardest to direct. There was the brilliant Richard O'Brien, with an unfinished musical called *They Came from Denton*. Brian Thomson, the set designer, contributed so much more than just the set. And Richard Hartley, the musical director, who worked brilliantly with O'Brien. It was a perfect combination—O'Brien would write the song, and Hartley would finesse it, making it blossom. Jim also needed a costume designer. The Royal Court gave him two phone numbers, and the first one he called was a twenty-four-year-old girl, Sue Blane, who had just been working at the Glasgow Citizens (repertory). Together, I called them "The Five."

Sue Blane Brian Thomson was a magician of design. He used to be called the Andy Warhol of Australia, but I think that's not high enough praise. He was a superb designer with a brilliant mind and was a lot of fun.

"One day, Richard mentioned to me that he had an idea for a musical. I said, 'I hope it's not religious.' And of course it's the only one that ended up with its own cult."

—Jim Sharman

As Richard put pen to paper to write his earliest draft of Rocky Horror, the '70s were in full swing. It was a time of great social change, musically and sexually, especially for Richard.

Richard O'Brien I was a recent father of my first child and out of work when I wrote the show. 1972 to '73 was a moment of change. Glam rock and overt sexuality was around, gay people were coming out, and there was a buzz in the air. There were certain parts of the world where we were a little bit more free to be ourselves. London was certainly one of them.

Tim Curry I didn't have any clue at the time of Richard's intense struggle with his sexuality. It makes sense.

Richard O'Brien Being gay back in the day, in my day, it was something you had to hide. Because you could go to prison for it. I always felt that I was living in no-man's-land. I never felt that I belonged anywhere. I was quite happy to be there. I wasn't tormented. If I hadn't been the way I was, Frank-N-Furter would never come to life. There would never be a *Rocky Horror* show. So, out of adversity came something good.

Chrissie Messenger In the early days of the 1970s, you didn't cross-dress. It just wasn't done. But Richard always had parties. I was invited to one when he was with [his second wife] Jane [Moss], and I went. There was a woman in a long black lace dress with long gray hair who kept smiling at me. She looked terribly familiar—it was Richard! The next time I saw him cross-dress, he was in a pink tutu. Quite different. Initially, he had to come out slowly, portraying a dignified older woman, which he did very well.

Richard O'Brien I remember the first time I went out in a frock and somebody said to me, "Oh, you're out of the closet." I said, "I may well have been in the closet, but the door was wide open."

Karen Tongson The early to mid-1970s was a time when people were grappling with the social movements and revolutionary efforts that emerged in the late '60s. This was a period of codifying what began as protest, trying to push it into our art, our world, and the way we lived. *Rocky* came at a time when the gay liberation movement, post-Stonewall, was in full swing, as well as other events like the Black Cat riots in Los Angeles.

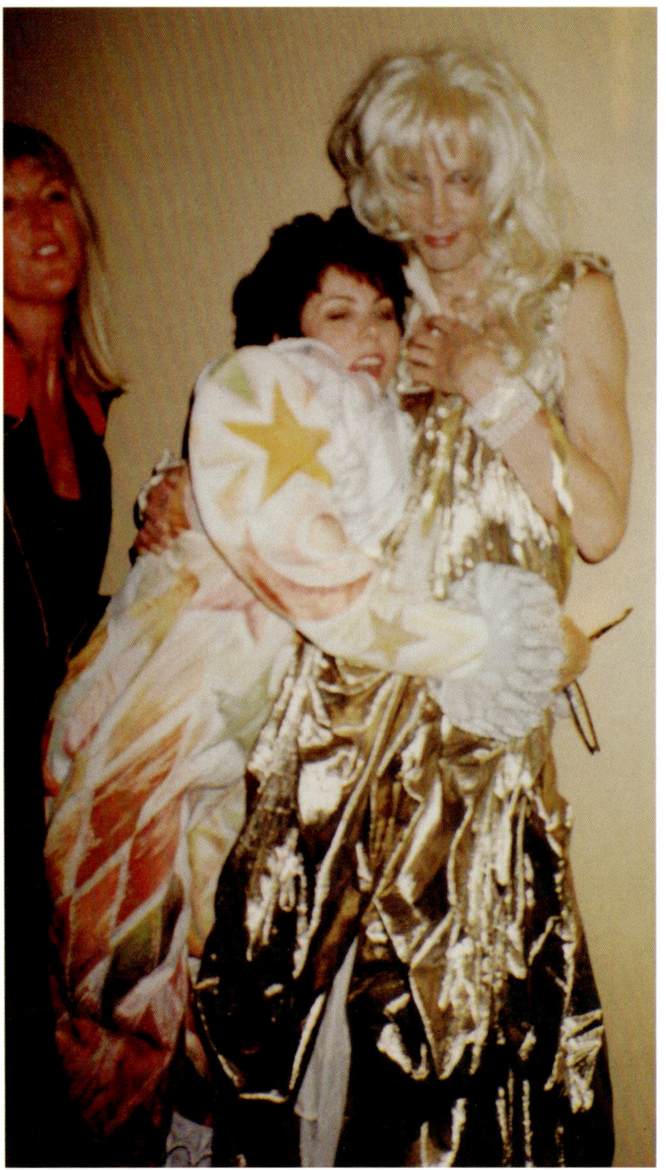

Richard with the legendary Ruby Wax.

Richard glamming it up around the house, London c. 1973.

"In 1973, *Rocky* was very indicative of people wanting to try and find a way that they could admit to their families about their sexual hopes and fantasies—the strong gay themes had never really been exploited in that way before, even in the 1970s."

—John Goldstone

Chrissie Messenger Richard paved the way and opened the door for so many people who must have been suffering with their sexuality and gender, just as he did. What got him through was his honesty and integrity.

Nell Campbell Homosexuality was only legalized in England in 1968. Only five years later, *The Rocky Horror Show* was a total celebration of homosexuality and bisexuality, trans cross-dressing. Richard, when he wrote it, had no idea it would have this effect on people. But that was the seed.

Belinda Sinclair I had friends who were gay but hadn't come out yet. *Rocky* helped a lot of people find the courage to come out. I'm so proud of that, and so proud of Richard for doing it, because I think the world would be different without *Rocky Horror*.

John Goldstone In 1973, *Rocky* was very indicative of people wanting to try and find a way that they could admit to their families about their sexual hopes and fantasies—the strong gay themes had never really been exploited in that way before, even in the 1970s.

Chrissie Messenger I remember when Richard must have come out to Jane. He was giving me a lift somewhere and said, "If I decided to change sex, would you still be my friend?" I said, "Yeah, because I'm your friend." He said, "Why doesn't my wife understand?"

Richard O'Brien *Rocky* fits in that little gap between glam rock and punk. I think, to some extent, *Rocky* was slightly influential on British punk. Malcolm McLaren used to come and see the show, and it had that punky, unprofessional vibe—professionally unprofessional, if you will.

Jack Black *Rocky Horror* has a punk rock energy—an attitude, a "fuck you" to the establishment. You can definitely see

Richard O'Brien, c. 1980.

the influence of the Sex Pistols and other punk rock bands in *Rocky Horror*'s veins.

Karen Tongson During the glam rock era, women were drawn to men who moved away from the traditional trappings of dominant, straight masculinity. These men allowed themselves to experience and express something beyond the restrictive privileges of that performance.

Richard O'Brien We came between glam rock and punk, hitting the zeitgeist for the gay community. Back then, pubs were full of openly gay men wearing porn mustaches, checkered shirts, and behaving like lumberjacks. Rocky was part of that moment of liberation, including women's liberation.

Nell Campbell My relationship with the glam rock movement of the '70s? I slept with most of them. But other than that, nothing.

The writing process for They Came from Denton High *(as it was then known) was a speedy affair once Richard, Jim, and Richard Hartley united as a creative tour de force. All they had to do was blend together each other's skills . . .*

Richard O'Brien Writing *Rocky* was almost like working on a jigsaw puzzle. I had written several of the songs before, and all I had to do was slot them in. I didn't start at the beginning and develop the plot from there. I started at both ends and then filled in the middle.

Jim Sharman I should have been impressed by Richard's ability to write songs and dialogue so fast, but there wasn't time. It's astonishing to think about what has come from those playful three weeks in the Theatre Upstairs at Sloane Square in London in 1973! It moved at quite a pace. Songs that were added during rehearsals certainly included the wedding scene, "Dammit Janet," "Touch-A, Touch-A, Touch Me," and the songs with Dr. Everett Scott.

Richard O'Brien I've little doubt that writing Frank was cathartic for me. There's something about that character—the rock and roll Cruella de Vil—that was appealing to me.

Tim Curry In writing *Rocky*, Richard reached up into the zeitgeist and brought down the most salient ingredients.

Richard Hartley *Rocky* is just *Frankenstein* with a twist. Except there's no twisting—it's rock 'n' roll. Richard and I listened to the same records when we were growing up, so we just put all the things we loved in. You can hear the influences: a bit of Chuck Berry, and a bit of Rolling Stones in "Sweet Transvestite." It's self-indulgent, but the songs aren't pastiche like the ones in Grease.

Richard O'Brien Quite why Frank wants a floor show, I've got no idea. It's the end of an evening. Everybody's tired. Why on earth he's doing this, there's no good, sound reason for it, but it does work.

Jim Sharman I told Richard we needed to establish Brad and Janet as the emotional center of the story—so that we actually care about them. Because, in *Rocky Horror*, the only character who truly changes is Janet.

Richard O'Brien I can't remember how I came up with the names for the characters. I grabbed them from the ether. Frank-N-Furter, obviously, that's an easy one. I'm amazed that I got away with it, really, because it really is childishly silly, isn't it? Riff Raff was called Joe Vitas before. Magenta was a color that I loved. Columbia? No idea.

Jim Sharman *Rocky Horror* is like a work of pop art. Richard, I remember, used to sketch cartoons, and I think in a way, he structured *Rocky Horror* like a cartoon.

Opposite: Richard Hartley and Richard O'Brien working their magic. Below: Richard O'Brien with Rocky Horror costume designer Sue Blane (left) and Nell Campbell (right).

Richard O'Brien There's not a great deal of dialogue in *Rocky*, actually. The longest speech is Frank's at the end. But it works quite well bare-bones.

Jim Sharman Every day, things changed. But the most dramatic change was my original suggestion to Richard that "Dammit Janet" needed two additional servants for Riff Raff. Richard came up with Magenta and Columbia—and once they were there, I also thought they were technically necessary for harmonies.

Richard O'Brien There was about five or six weeks of getting the show together and then a three-week rehearsal. I was writing songs overnight for different characters. It was probably 60 percent finished before rehearsals.

Richard Hartley What's remarkable is that Richard wrote most of the songs the night before we needed them.

Richard O'Brien "Super Heroes"—I had that song just sitting in a drawer. "I'm Going Home" was sitting in the drawer. Brad's song "Once in a While" was sitting in a drawer. I just decided to use them.

Jim Sharman Between Richard coming from New Zealand, myself, designer Brian Thomson, and Nell Campbell coming from Australia, we all brought a certain irreverence. We weren't caught up in the class system, and maybe that rebellious desire to change things helped shape *Rocky Horror*.

Nell Campbell I've always considered *The Rocky Horror Show* to be slightly antipodean. Richard's from New Zealand, Brian, Jim, and I from Australia.

"*Rocky Horror* is the only musical written with a crayon."

—Richard O'Brien

"*Rocky Horror* is a movie about movies. And the song 'Science Fiction/Double Feature' is a song about movies, a movie about movies. There's something about the way that chorus kicks in—it reminds me of being eighteen years old in a movie theater, the smell of popcorn, the soda, drunk people screaming, and the rice. Let me tell you, in *Rocky Horror*, you will find rice in places you never thought you'd find it."

—Trixie Mattel

ICA
4 July -
12 August
RICHARD O'BRIEN'S
ROGET'S
THESAURUS

CHAPTER 2

A WILD AND UNTAMED THING

With the stage show nowhere near complete, and armed with only a handful of tunes, time was quickly ticking toward the show's opening night at the Royal Court's Theatre Upstairs. The creators and collaborators had to be quick to lure their perfect Frank-N-Furter—and other unconventional conventionalists—in order to be ready. Thankfully, they were among friends and sane persons. Well, sort of . . .

Summer 1973. As Jim Sharman and Richard O'Brien worked together with Richard Hartley to transform Richard's words into a cohesive sound and vision, costume designer Sue Blane and set designer Brian Thomson got to work creating the iconic look of Rocky*...*

Jim Sharman The stage show was created in a very playful way, with a lot of improvisation, and many people contributed to what it became. The goal was always to make something completely different from what people expected from a musical.

Richard Hartley For Richard, this was a big moment—his show, written and being put on by one of the most celebrated musical theater directors in London at the time. Jim had had a massive hit with *Jesus Christ Superstar* in London. Richard and I were just starting out in our careers, but Jim was already quite the celebrity.

Richard O'Brien I first met Michael White, who became the producer of *Rocky*, in 1973. He kindly gave us £2,000 for our fringe theater event. That was a lot of money back then—about £20,000 today. It was a huge risk.

Jim Sharman At the start, we took the horror side of the show very seriously, combining it with eroticism, perversity, and a real sense of danger.

Jeffrey Weinstock The original stage production came together very quickly. There was about a three-month period for designing, casting, and assembling everything, followed by three weeks of rehearsals. They had two days of previews, during which they made a lot of script changes.

Jim Sharman We were always looking for new ways to present the play. We were exploring radical, experimental approaches—taking inspiration from Eastern European theater, where the audience might look down on the action from above in a tiny space. We didn't treat Richard's play as conventional theater; we treated it as something entirely new.

Richard O'Brien Brian Thomson, the set designer, had an architectural degree and was a huge fan of Mondrian's minimalist approach. For our first set, we had almost nothing—just a white canvas stretched over a frame that mimicked a cinema screen, and a black box covered with black felt. On one side, we had some old-fashioned switches to represent the lab, and that was it. There wasn't even a car onstage. Brad and Janet would mime driving, and when they got out, the "car" would disappear. It was a bit magical.

Brian Thomson One day we were all sitting around wondering how we were going to handle the staging. We wanted a hardware science-fiction look but could hardly afford it on a set design budget of $500. Suddenly I remembered an image I had stored away. A few months before, I had gone to the cinema and saw this usherette selling ice cream on the side of the stage with a spotlight shining on her. I thought it was one of the most theatrical things I'd ever seen. I suggested that "Science Fiction," the show's opening number, be sung by an usherette. The setting of the show just evolved from there.

Opposite: Richard with Rocky *producer Michael White, c. 1973. Right: Patricia Quinn as the Usherette in the original London production.*

Tim Curry in Sue Blane's original costume design.

Nell Campbell Brian Thomson was given £500 to do the set. Even in 1973, that was very little money. Most of everything was borrowed.

Sue Blane Jim and I decided to dress Tim in underwear for the role of Frank. The idea was that Frank-N-Furter never leaves his castle and doesn't need to dress socially, so he should be comfortable in what he looks good in: underwear. This way, we wouldn't have to spend money on dresses or coats. A corset worked beautifully for this.

Tim Curry Sue Blane I'd worked with before in a theater in Glasgow, Scotland. I had worn the corset before in a show we did together called *The Maids*, by Jean Genet. So I was used to wearing that. It didn't bother me much. It took me a while to get used to platform shoes with four-inch heels. But I got the measure of that pretty quickly and stomped around quite happily.

Sue Blane There wasn't much money for costumes, but I found some wonderful pieces, including old donations of underwear from people who had passed away. One piece, a 1920s long-line corset with whalebone, stood out. During the fitting, I held it up, and Tim wasn't sure about it. I turned it around so that the curve of the corset was on his hip instead of over his breast. He looked fantastic in it.

Patricia Quinn I do remember that during the dress rehearsal, which was in a room, Tim put on his high heels for the first time. That was a pivotal moment for him. It was also the first time I had my ice cream tray onstage. Since I'd worked as an usher in real life at the Classic Cinema in Notting Hill Gate, I instantly knew how to play it.

Sue Blane The inspiration for the high heels, I can't quite remember. It just seemed obvious that Tim should look sexy, so we went for the full look. The heels weren't particularly high.

Tim Curry I was fine with Frank's flamboyance. But even with a song like "Sweet Transvestite," it didn't quite click with me when I read it that he was going to be wearing feminine clothes and high heels. I thought he was going to have a lab coat . . . And then I saw the costume design!

Sue Blane Riff Raff was intentionally made to look like someone who'd never washed his shirt or waistcoat—or even himself.

Richard O'Brien I remember being told that Riff Raff should have on dirty underpants. And I can see the funniness in it. But I absolutely refused. I put my foot down with that. I wasn't going onstage with yellow underpants!

Sue Blane The influence for the costumes came from the strange outfits I was beginning to see around Kensington, Chelsea, and the King's Road, as glam rock started to kick in. Vivienne Westwood or Malcolm McLaren may have had the same influences I was seeing. I don't know if *Rocky Horror* had any impact on them, but I'm sure they would have seen it.

Jeffrey Weinstock *Rocky* emerged right at the moment punk was taking shape. Sue Blane has said she doesn't want to take credit for inventing punk, but the aesthetic she created—ripped fishnet stockings, wild-colored hair, and glitter—was very much in line with what was developing in the punk scene.

Richard O'Brien Nell's dress sense played a big role in shaping the British punk look. When Sue Blane designed Columbia's costume, it was very much inspired by what Nell used to wear herself on the street—almost exactly what she wore.

Nell Campbell When people see the show and the film, everyone looks so iconic. It is hard to imagine anyone else but Sue Blane creating these iconic looks. She had a budget of just £400. Hundreds of thousands—if not millions—of people have dressed in costumes created by Sue.

"Frank is this self-obsessed, selfish diva that wants everything for themself and has absolutely no interest in anybody else. It's a very liberating character to play. How much of me is in Frank, you tell me."

—Richard O'Brien

Following pages: A showcase of Sue Blane's genius costume design from the original London production. Left: Richard O'Brien (Riff Raff), Tim Curry (Frank-N-Furter), and Patricia Quinn (Magenta). Right: Patricia and Nell Campbell (Columbia).

Above: Tim Curry. Opposite: Tim as Dr. Frank-N-Furter in the original London production.

We meet at last! Tim Curry's inspired casting as Frank-N-Furter has remained iconic for more than half a century. He breathed life into a psychopathic character obsessed with lust, sex, and glory. Ladies and gentlemen, how do you do?

Tim Curry I lived in a tiny, crappy apartment on Paddington Street opposite Baker Street Underground Station in London. Two doors down was a gym. One day, I was out on the sidewalk, and I bumped into Richard. He was coming out of the gym. I said, "What were you doing in the gym?" And he said, "I'm looking for a muscleman who can sing." I said, "Really? Why do you need him to sing?" And then he told me he had written this musical that he was going to put on at the Royal Court Theatre. And I said, "That's great." And then I was asked to audition for it. And I did. I read the script and thought, "Boy, if this works, it's going to be a smash."

Richard O'Brien Frank is this self-obsessed, selfish diva that wants everything for themself and has absolutely no interest in anybody else. It's a very liberating character to play. How much of me is in Frank, you tell me.

Jeffrey Weinstock Frank is essentially Dionysus—the god of passion, the god of unleashed sexuality. Tim Curry's performance is so dynamic, so over-the-top, and so sensationalistic that it becomes a wave of sexuality that washes over the audience, sweeping up everyone—male or female—in its wake. For some reason, even heteronormative men can find something attractive about Frank—because Frank isn't human.

Richard Hartley My first impression of Tim Curry was that he was quiet, dry, and witty—a real gentleman. Nothing like Frank-N-Furter in real life, but that's what makes him a great actor.

Tim Curry Frank-N-Furter was this mad scientist, so when I first read for the part, I read it with a German accent because he was called Frank-N-Furter. Then, one day I was on a bus in London and a woman in front of me said to her friend, "Do you live in town, or do you have a house in the country?" And I thought that's how Frank ought to sound—like the Queen. So that's how that happened. And it stuck.

Richard Hartley I do remember Tim having a bit of a German accent in rehearsals, which wasn't completely German because he wasn't quite sure.

Tim Curry Joan Crawford was my main inspiration for Frank-N-Furter. He's kind of an extremist, Frank. He says he's a transvestite transsexual, whatever that means. I don't play him as a transsexual. But he's a fairly complex guy. He just takes anything he can get. He's not fussy, really. Though I think he's something of a wham-bam-thank-you-ma'am.

Sue Blane The fact that Jim and Richard had already cast Tim Curry as Frank-N-Furter was music to my ears. I adored working with him in Glasgow in *The Maids* a year earlier.

Jim Sharman When Tim sang "Tutti Frutti" at the audition, we didn't need to see anyone else. He nailed it in one. He had every quality the role required. Finding the character took a little longer—Tim experimented a lot before settling into Frank. I certainly encouraged him—and probably cajoled him—into pushing beyond what was expected. I had a habit of insisting people go beyond themselves, beyond the norm, beyond expectations. It added an element of danger—so that the audience never quite knew what would happen next.

Jeffrey Weinstock What Tim Curry gives Frank is charisma. He manages to be exuberant, expressive, and lustful while still having moments of sweetness, vulnerability, and humor. It's a tour-de-force performance, and I think it's the reason the entire *Rocky* cult exists.

Nell Campbell If you take Tim out of the equation, would the show have been the roaring success? I'm sure it would have been a success, but Tim was so brilliant it guaranteed it. Every night people went nuts over his performance, and everybody fancied him so much.

With Tim Curry clearly born to raise hell with his Frank-N-Furter, the pressure was on Jim and Richard to find equally perfect actors to penetrate the roles of Magenta, Brad, Janet, Columbia, Rocky, the Criminologist, and—bless his soul—Eddie.

Richard O'Brien Casting for the original *Rocky Horror* was a special experience for me because it was the first time I was on the other side of the fence, sitting next to the director while people came in to audition. It felt delightful to be there, watching it all unfold.

Jim Sharman When actors write musicals, they tend to imagine themselves in the central role. But I always saw Richard as Riff Raff—because of his connection to Nosferatu and his physical look.

Richard O'Brien All I wanted to do was play Eddie: pop out of a Coke machine, sing a rock and roll song, and pop back into the Coke machine. I was really nervous about the whole thing. But I respected Jim Sharman, and since he felt I should play Riff Raff, I had to go along with him.

Patricia Quinn When I arrived in London from Belfast at seventeen, I came to be an actress. I was playing parts, working in theater. I had done a play at the Royal Court Theatre Upstairs the year before, called *AC/DC*, by Heathcote Williams. So, they knew me at the Royal Court. Gillian Diamond, the casting director, got in touch with me and said, "You should audition for this musical."

Patricia Quinn c. 1973.

Nell Campbell as Columbia.

Julie Covington, the original Janet Weiss.

Richard Hartley We made an interesting choice for *Rocky's* (Rayner Bourton) voice. We decided he should sing in falsetto because, being newly "born," his voice hadn't fully broken yet. Richard didn't quite agree with me on that, but I thought dramatically it worked—it created this contrast of a high voice coming out of this muscular guy.

Richard O'Brien Before rehearsals, Jim told me Marianne Faithfull wanted to be part of the show and asked if I could write a part for her. I revised Columbia's role, adding lines and creating the character of Magenta. When I finished, I asked Jim where Marianne was, and he said she had gone to India to "find her guru." That was the end of that. Thankfully, Patricia Quinn stepped in and performed the role beautifully.

Patricia Quinn I was told to turn up at the audition with a rock and roll song. There was no play, and there was no script. I thought, "I don't sing rock and roll!" So, I went to the audition and saw these guys: Richard was wearing a leopard-skin jacket, and Jim Sharman, the Australian director, in white platforms, and Richard Hartley, who had frizzy curly hair, just like mine at the time. They didn't look like your usual BBC crowd. They said, "Let's hear it." So I started singing a Jessie Matthews number from the 1930s, "Over My Shoulder"—doing high kicks as I sang. When I finished, they looked at me and said, "We've got a song you could sing, called "Science Fiction/Double Feature."

After the audition, I skipped with joy down the King's Road, thinking, "I knew I had to be part of it." Within half an hour of getting home, my agent called and said, "They want you." But then he added, "It's £18 a week for three weeks at the Royal Court Upstairs. And you haven't seen the script yet." I said, "I don't care about the script. I've heard this song!" He replied, "You're probably not going to like the script, so make sure you read it before you make any decisions." When I got the script, it wasn't very appetizing. The character of Magenta had about four lines, but she had that song—the opening usherette song—which I was determined to perform. I insisted on doing it.

Nell Campbell and Patricia Quinn.

Richard O'Brien Nell, or Little Nell, came onto our radar as an Australian. In the '60s, Australians flocked to Great Britain, particularly to Earl's Court, nicknamed Kangaroo Valley. Australians like Nell had no inhibitions. She came over in that wave and started cleaning for Jim Sharman. I remember the first time I saw her, she was sitting on her bum outside his kitchen door waiting for us to arrive so she could go in and do the cleaning. She was just perfect. She had such joy.

Nell Campbell In 1971, aged nineteen, I lived in a squat near St. Pancras Station. Alongside busking, I worked in a little café called Smalls and was bored out of my mind. I often took over the sound system, playing music from the '20s, '30s, and '40s, and tap-danced on the tabletop in an outfit inspired by Ruby Keeler. One day, I was tap-dancing in this café when in walked Jim Sharman, Richard O'Brien, and Richard Hartley to get coffee. Earlier that day, Jim had told Richard the play needed to add an extra servant role to the script for harmonies and backup [singing]. While [I was] tap-dancing on the table, Jim looked at me, turned to Richard, and said, "There's your servant." For once, I didn't have to sleep with anyone to get a role. It's the first and last time that's happened.

Jim Sharman Everyone brought their own histories to the show, and those histories were fascinating. When casting, I wasn't just looking for actors with technical skill—I was looking in their eyes, asking, "Is this an interesting person? What history are they bringing?" Everyone brought heaps.

Nell Campbell Jim Sharman was after original characters, personalities, people with street cred and something unusual about them. That's how we were cast! At the first rehearsals, it became clear that only a few of the cast had good voices.

Richard Hartley We had three incredible voices: Richard, Julie, and Tim. The rest were . . . an acquired taste.

Patricia Quinn Julie Covington was the original Janet. She had just done *Evita*. She could really sing. Richard brought in a new song for her overnight called "Touch-A, Touch-A, Touch Me, I Wanna Be Dirty." Julie Covington said, "I'm not singing that, it's disgusting!" And I said, "I agree, that's outrageous. I want to be dirty!" But she sang it anyway.

With each actor perfectly suited to their character—including Rayner Bourton as Rocky, Julie Covington as Janet, and Chris Malcolm as Brad—Jim and Richard had found their Denton-bound cast of geeks and misfits. Now it was time to get their act together and rehearse.

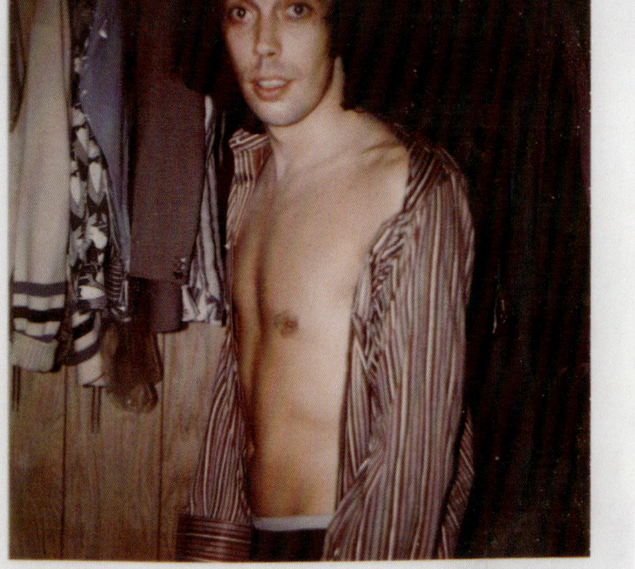

Jim Sharman (left) and Tim Curry (right) during rehearsals for the London production.

Jeffrey Weinstock There was a buzz around *The Rocky Horror Show* almost as soon as rehearsals began.

Jim Sharman During rehearsals, one of the first things that changed was the title. I didn't think that *They Came from Denton High* had the right ring to it. I suggested the title *The Rocky Horror Show* on a simple principle: It's a rock and roll horror show—so why not just call it what it is?

Nell Campbell There was only two months between *The Unseen Hand* finishing its run and *Rocky Horror* opening. We had the three-week rehearsal. Much of *The Rocky Horror Show* was actually written during the rehearsal.

Richard Hartley I was there throughout rehearsals for the first run at the Royal Court, as the pianist and musical director. The atmosphere was fantastic—no egos, just a group of people fully committed to making the show work. Everyone quickly found their characters. Some people naturally fit into their roles, like Patricia Quinn, who already had that incredible voice. But it was a true ensemble piece from the start.

Tim Curry First rehearsals were a really good time, very creative. I remember reaching a crisis point fairly early on because I would snap out an order to somebody and they wouldn't quite jump to it. I stopped and had a rather small tantrum. The rest of the cast were all good about that—acting is a very competitive sport. And you have to take it on like a prize fight. And I've lost a few in my time.

Richard Hartley I do remember Tim becoming more assertive during rehearsals. He felt that to properly embody the character, he needed real authority. At one point, he snapped and said, "If you want me to be powerful, I have to have power." And honestly, he was right. He didn't want Frank to be a campy caricature.

Richard O'Brien In rehearsals, we had Julie Covington as Janet, who later had a huge hit with "Don't Cry for Me Argentina" before Elaine

> **"Everyone brought their own histories to the show, and those histories were fascinating. When casting, I wasn't just looking for actors with technical skill—I was looking in their eyes, asking, 'Is this an interesting person? What history are they bringing?' "**
>
> **—Jim Sharman**

Above: Nell Campbell.
Opposite: The London cast: (left to right) Nell Campbell, Richard O'Brien, Patricia Quinn, and Jonathan Adams as the Narrator.

"First rehearsals were a really good time, very creative. I remember reaching a crisis point fairly early on because I would snap out an order to somebody and they wouldn't quite jump to it. I stopped and had a rather small tantrum. The rest of the cast were all good about that—acting is a very competitive sport. And you have to take it on like a prize fight. And I've lost a few in my time."

—Tim Curry

Paige in *Evita*. When *Rocky* became a success, it ran in London for seven years. Tim played it in Los Angeles for about eight months in '74. And who replaced him? Paul Jabara—the very actor I was meant to replace in *Superstar*. A nice full-circle moment.

Nell Campbell For the Royal Court Theatre Upstairs, we had a three-week rehearsal period and a three-week run, to start. Everyone involved was paid £18 a week for those six weeks.

Jeffrey Weinstock During rehearsals, Jim Sharman encouraged ad-libbing, and if something worked, they kept it. Amazingly, there wasn't a finalized *Rocky Horror* script until the first preview.

Patricia Quinn Jim didn't really "direct" in the traditional sense. He had two expressions: One was a slight smile, like, "Hmm, I like that." The other was a neutral look, signaling "That's it, we've changed direction." That was it.

Jim would often turn to Richard and say, "I want a song for Magenta, Riff Raff, and Columbia now." He wanted a dance song and a dance for us. Richard went home that night and worked on it. The next day, he came back with "The Time Warp." Most of the songs Richard wrote overnight and brought them to rehearsals.

Richard Hartley Most of the songs drive the plot forward, and they're constructed like pop songs—verse, chorus, maybe a middle eight. When we arranged them, we approached them like we were making catchy pop songs, not creating musical statements. We wanted them to sound like songs you could imagine on a record.

When new songs were added, Richard would work on them in the evening, then come around to my flat near the Royal Court. He'd play them on guitar and ask, "Do you think this works?" We'd discuss it—maybe tweak a chord change—then I'd record it on my little cassette machine. After that, I'd write out the chords and melody so we could teach it to the cast.

Our musical inspiration at the time was the Rolling Stones. The guitar riffs in the songs Richard was writing had that feel and were a bit raunchier. Keith Richards's famous phrase "Solos come and go, but a riff is forever" is what we tried to capture in "Sweet Transvestite" and the floor show—guitar riffs were an essential part of the songwriting.

TIME WARP

RIFF RAFF

CUE: "IT SEEMS LIKE ONLY YESTERDAY SINCE HE WENT.... WHERE? TO PIECES!"

VAMP — A — (GUIT.) — RIFF RAFF — IT'S A- — A — STOUND-ING. —

3 TIME IS FLEET-ING — B — G — MAD- NESS

6 TAKES ITS TOL... — D — A — ...S-TEN CLOSE- LY

COLUMBIA MAGENTA — RIFF RAFF — DO IT! I RE-

56 WARP,

A — WHEN —

59 ...O THE VOID WOULD BE

-2-

22 B♭ — CHORUS — E♭ — OO, OO, OO WILL BUILD A CREA-TURE; — Cm — CHORUS — BOOM, BOOM,

25 A♭ — BOOM SEE AN-DROIDS FIGHT-ING; — B♭ — CHORUS — OO, OO, OO — E♭ — BRAD AND

28 Cm — JAN-ETS — CHORUS — BOOM, BOOM, BOOM — A♭ — ANNE FRAN-CIS STARS — B♭ — IN; — CHORUS — OO, OO,

31 E♭ — OO FOR-BID-EN PLA- NET — Cm — OH, OH, OH — A♭ — OH —

34 AT THE LATE NIGHT DOU-BLE FEA-TURE — B♭ — PIC-TURE

37 ① E♭ — SHOW — D♭ — OH! — A♭ — OH! — B♭sus — OH! — B♭ — I KNEW

41 ② E♭ — SHOW I WAN-NA GO, — Cm — OH, OH — A♭ (DIM. POCO A POCO)

44 TO THE LATE NIGHT DOU-BLE FEA-TURE PIC-TURE — B♭

E♭ — Cm — A♭

FRANKENSTEIN PLACE

JANET

CUE: "BEAUTIFUL WOMAN, AND YOU MAY NEVER COME BACK!

START VAMP UNDER LAUGHTER

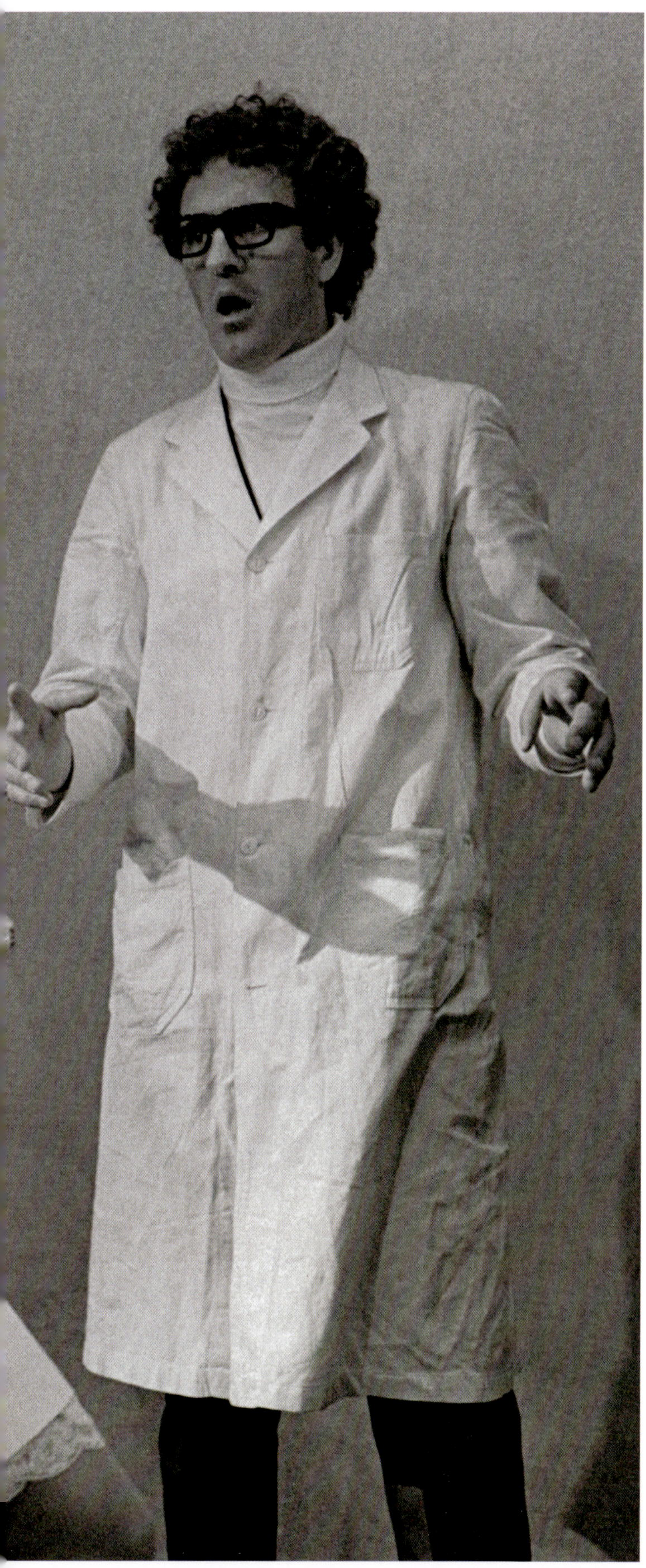

John Goldstone For me, Richard Hartley was key to early live shows. I remember them vividly because of him and his band above the stage. And there was a kind of energy that he created with that music and the way he transposed it from Richard's ideas.

Richard Hartley Richard [O'Brien] has a knack for simplicity in his songs. With *Rocky*, because the lyrics are so witty and poetic, if the music was too complicated, it would fight against them. His skill is in creating something simple, memorable, and perfectly fitted to the lyrics.

Richard O'Brien It became apparent that Julie Covington needed a song. She was known for her voice. It seemed silly not to give her one. So, that's how "Touch Me" came about.

Nell Campbell One day, Jim told Richard, "I think Janet needs a song for her sexual awakening. Richard, could you please go home?" The next day, Richard showed up and sang "Touch Me." Richard would literally go home and write another perfect song. So many songs were written and added during that three-week rehearsal, because Jim had a great instinct for where he needed things.

Richard O'Brien The rehearsal period at the Theatre Upstairs was joyous. It was at the top of the building, with a stand-up piano for rehearsals. As someone sang and learned their song, the notes tinkled through the air. There was a feeling of joy, silliness, and fun as you walked through the building. It was a serious theater most of the time, so having fun like this was delightful, and that sense of joy permeated the space.

After three weeks of rehearsals, frantic rewriting sessions, and preparing the costumes and derelict cinema aesthetic in the theater, Rocky Horror *was finally ready to pull up his golden speedos. The world premiere of* The Rocky Horror Show *at the Royal Court's Theatre Upstairs began at 10:30 p.m. on June 19, 1973, after previews the two previous nights. In its June 23, 1973, review of the show,* The Guardian *wrote, "Richard O'Brien's musical fantasy achieves the rare feat of being witty and erotic at the same time." Take your seats.*

The original London cast: (left to right) Patricia Quinn (Magenta), Nell Campbell (Columbia), Julie Covington (Janet), and Christopher Malcolm (Brad).

THE ROYAL COURT THEATRE UPSTAIRS PRESENTS...

19.6.73

THE ROCKY HORROR SHOW BY RICHARD O'BRIEN

SOMETHING FOR EVERYONE

Opposite: Richard O'Brien designed and drew the original playbill art, which then turned into the poster for the show, shown here displayed on the front of the Royal Theatre (above).

Above: Unwrapping Frank's man with blond hair and a tan (Rayner Bourton). Right: Tim Curry, London production. Following pages: Charles Atlas has nothing on Frank when it comes to making a man.

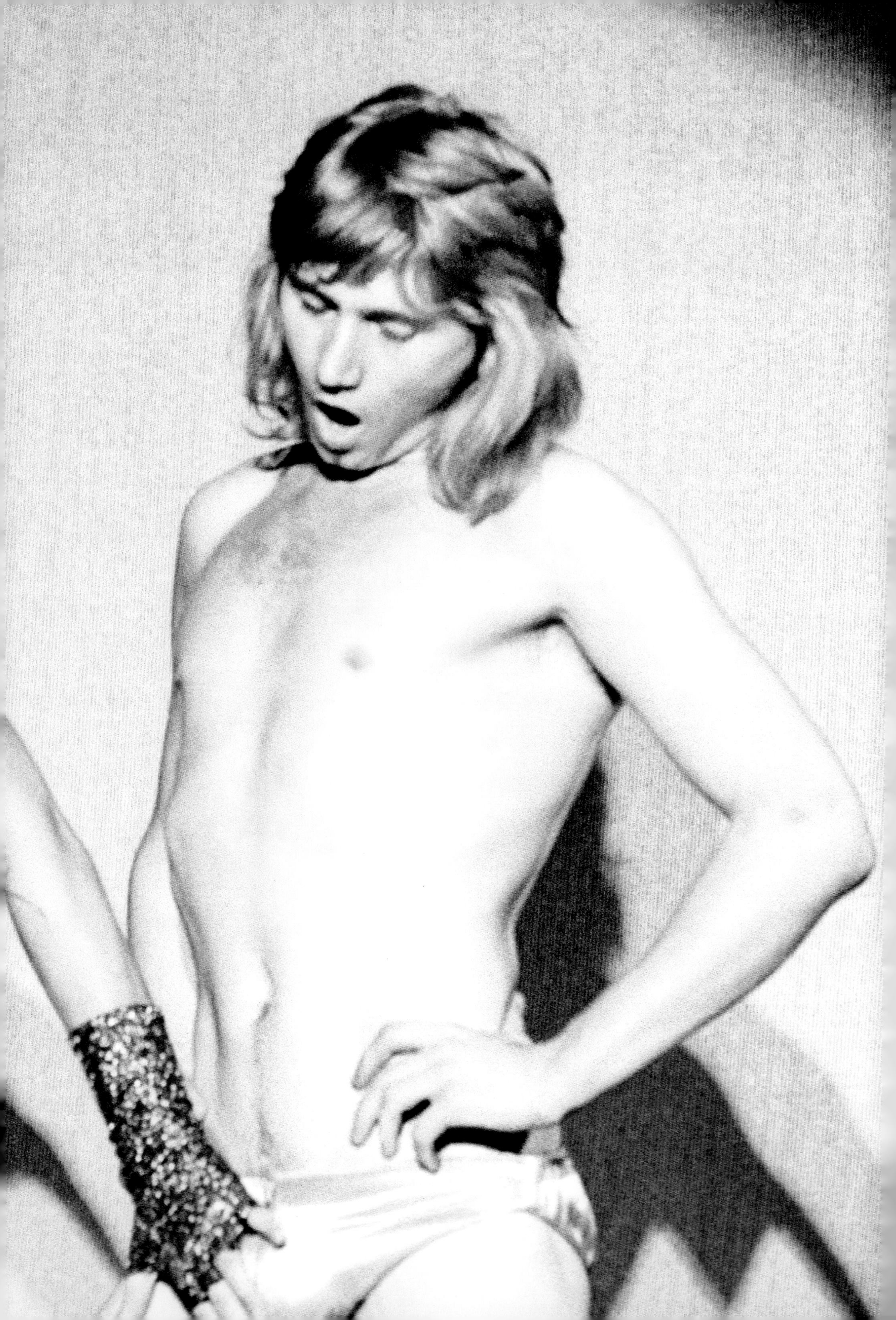

Richard O'Brien A three-week run is wonderful. It's just enough. You're not getting bored of it; things stay fresh. You never got a chance to think, "Not tonight. Not again."

Sue Blane I remember the dress rehearsal, because I hadn't really appreciated just how hysterically funny it was. The panache—it was like an explosion of energy. And the sound was incredible. It was a fabulous score. The rehearsals had been fun, but it hadn't quite jelled for me until the dress rehearsal.

Richard O'Brien On the first preview, I was nervous. We'd had a dress rehearsal in the afternoon and a break before the show, so I went to a pub for a drink, then had another, and ended up having one too many. When I returned, I quickly realized it was a mistake. I was struggling to keep up and sweating, my nerves running wild. But then we got to "Over at the Frankenstein Place," and when they sang the line "Over at the Frankenstein Place," the audience laughed. That laughter brought a huge flood of relief—I knew then that it wasn't going to go too badly, and that everything would be all right. If they were laughing at that, they'd laugh at anything!

Richard Hartley We initially thought we'd play for just three weeks, but it sold out quickly. The reviews were fantastic. Within a week, we knew we had something special. It was the right show at the right time. It appealed across all demographics, even though that word wasn't commonly used at the time. It had a mixed audience, and the Royal Court, being on King's Road, was the perfect venue with its liberal arts, fashion, and music vibe.

Jeffrey Weinstock The first performances of *Rocky Horror* at the Royal Court had to start late, but the theater staff didn't want to stay that late. So the production team had to improvise. That's where they came up with the idea of having an usher, played by Patricia Quinn, who would welcome the audience and help seat them—although not always in the way they expected!

Nell Campbell Jim made me, Richard O'Brien, Patricia, and Paddy O'Hagan [Eddie] the ushers—the ones who weren't onstage right away. We had to wear these hideous synthetic nylon jackets and translucent masks—very sinister. Jim Sharman immediately dubbed us the Phantom Ghouls. We stood at the top of the stairs where the audience would arrive, never speaking. We'd silently encourage them to hand us their tickets, take them, examine them, and either point or suddenly stare at people. Jim credits the Phantom Ghouls with creating the atmosphere of a haunted house.

Patricia Quinn At the Theatre Upstairs, there was no curtain, so I began the show sitting onstage with my ice cream tray under a piece of netting. The audience would come in and poke at the netting, trying to figure out what it was. They weren't quite sure.

Chrissie Messenger I remember the opening night very well. My ex-boyfriend [Mick Jagger] tried to get in. There were quite a few famous people who tried to get in too, including Elliott Gould.

Richard Hartley The Royal Court was such a small space. You could watch the audience. I'd never really seen a theater audience react that way before—it was something completely different. At the time, I just thought we were having fun, playing to full houses. But looking back, it was something special.

Sue Blane The opening-night reception was fabulous. I went away to another job but kept getting all these reports from people in London saying, "You have no idea what's going on. You can't get a ticket for it. It's absolutely amazing." Before I knew it, it was a huge hit and was going to transfer to King's Road. Remarkable. Never looked back.

Nell Campbell I was absolutely surprised by the phenomenal success of the play when it opened. The glowing reviews were in the papers the next morning.

A rave review from the Evening Standard, *June 26, 1973.*

THE OTHER THEATRE : Naseem Khan

Highly satirical—Frankenstein takes on a new bent

FRANKIE and Janet : Sexual spoof

THE FIRST NIGHT of **The Rocky Horror Show** at the Theatre Upstairs was marked by thunder, lightning and torrential rain. Strictly speaking, the Royal Court should feel indebted to God for those aptly sinister off-stage noises—unless they were intended as signs of divine disapproval at a show of joyful sexual irreverence.

"Don't dream it, do it," goes one of the show's lyrics. And indeed the cast does it all; all ways, all combinations—joyfully, satirically, wittily and musically. The Rocky Horror Show takes you on a trip and leaves your libido to look after itself.

It starts the minute you enter the Theatre Upstairs. You thought you were going to the theatre? Wrong. What you are in is a rather seedy cinema. Large screen before you, rows of sagging red seats, ushers (though with strangely fixed grins) lighting your way. "The Sloane Cinema," says a large placard, "regrets the incovenience caused to patrons during renovations. Modern 3-screen cinema will open shortly."

It's the cinema that provides The Rocky Horror Show with its references—nostalgic, affectionate references to the days of the banal giants and the simple life they showed.

Brad and Janet are two nice straight American kids marooned on a lonely road by a burst tyre. Following a handy light coming from the Frankenstein place, they find themselves embroiled in bizarre skullduggery. Sinister servants introduce them to the Doctor. But it's no Frankenstein that Mary Shelley would have ever recognised. This one is a transvestite, dumped on Earth from the planet Transexual in the galaxy Transylvania. He/she is bent on creating the perfect youth and, it so happens, that that night is unveiling night. (A discarded model, rock'n' roll style, is kept in the ice-box.)

More shocks face the young couple from the randy Frankie and the staff, all designed to give them "sensual daydreams to treasure for ever." But in the tradition of the best old movies, tables are turned, the outsider startles the field, and it all ends in a trans-sexual freakout. Even the gimlet-eyed government investigator kicks his fishnet legs from his wheelchair like a liberated lamb.

Jim Sharman has staged this great spoof opera with bold imagination. The cast swings from the ceiling, leaps along catwalks, tumbles down ramps, hitting you with songs that range from mock country and western to good rock. And if there were a female version of the Oscar, Tim Curry should get it for his performance as the kinky doctor. Elegant, disdainful, he stalks through the action dressed in impeccable corset and high-heeled shoes.

The script, by Richard O'Brien (who also wrote music and lyrics) has a sure ear for the homely banalities. "I made you, and I can break you," hisses Frankie of the mutinous Rocky. The mixture of elements—movies, pop, sci-fi, will undoubtedly remind people of Sam Shepard. But it's different. Shepard comments through his material; O'Brien has created a satirical and affectionate send-up that, unlike Rocky, remains well within control.

At the King's Head things are somewhat quieter. **The Enlightenment of the Strawberry Gardener**, on at lunchtime, is one of those mad modern fables about bureaucracy.

It's set in the faceless office of Ombudsman Bullfrog where he sits testily waiting for the the public's complaints. Mr Pike, however, is not one of the importunate people who irritate him to violence. Pike, a mild, worried man, is willing to search for a compromise. He's worried with good cause, since his house is slowly sinking below municipal water and his womenfolk are taking to the boats and leaving for ever.

Don Haworth's play is assured, witty and slightly quaint; it wins on stage against all odds since it is essentially a simple confrontation across an office desk. Both performances hold the attention well—John Blythe as the fleshy, genial ombudsman, with violence just below the surface and Peter John as the sad strawberry gardener who at last sees the light. The direction by Walter Hall is able and intelligent.

Where to go

● **THEATRE UPSTAIRS: Royal Court, Sloane Square, S.W.1. (730 2554). (Sloane Square Tube). The Rocky Horror Show, by Richard O'Brien, directed by Jim Sharman. (Ends July 14.) Mon.-Fri. 10 p.m., Sat. 11 p.m. 80p, students 40p.**

● **KINGS HEAD: 115 Upper Street, N.1. (226 1916). (Angel Tube). The Enlightenment of the Strawberry Gardener, by Don Haworth, directed by Walter Hall. Presented by Basement Theatre. Tues.-Sat. 1.15. 30p. M'ship 60p; first visit free.**

Left: Frank (Tim Curry) admires his work (Rayner Bourton as Rocky).
Opposite: The sweet transvestite scales the ladder of success.

"It is a musical comedy so long as the people are laughing, what more could I want? . . . If I'm standing at the back of the theater and I hear that audience roar with laughter and that band's cooking, I couldn't be happier."

—Richard O'Brien

Jeffrey Weinstock By the time previews started, the press was already excited. The reviews were overwhelmingly positive—it was praised for being both witty and sexy, which isn't always an easy balance to strike.

Jim Sharman I don't think we knew quite what to expect when the show first opened. But at the previews, rock stars and famous artists were fighting over tickets. We suddenly realized something had happened. Plus, a bit of thunder and lightning on opening night added to the moment.

Chrissie Messenger When I went to the show on opening night, I was really surprised. It was shocking, even in the supposed swinging '70s! It was not a family show. It was still a conservative time, especially for women. I remember when Julie sang "Touch Me" and I thought, "Oh my God, women can't say that." It was way ahead of its time.

Nell Campbell Vincent Price and Coral Browne came to our opening night, and an incredible storm raged outside. Can you imagine a better omen than having Vincent Price there? A raging electrical storm with thunder and lightning. People ask why it became a hit—well, right there.

Richard O'Brien Vincent Price was sitting in the audience under the skylight. The lightning flashed and lit him up. I thought: "Fuck me, that's a good omen!" The theater was packed and sweaty. There wasn't a spare inch. We had one microphone hanging down from the ceiling, and it would swing past the audience's heads.

Richard Hartley There two moments from the original play that stand out for me. At the Frankenstein Place, the original set made it feel like the audience was entering a cinema. There was a white cinema screen, and overhead, Frankenstein Place had this cramped, almost upstairs-theater feel, which was tough considering we only had a couple of lights and a microphone. But when Riff Raff appeared, he would be lit from the side, standing on a high chair at the top of the screen. The light hit him in such a way that it really enhanced the moment—his skin, the whole thing was striking. The audience could feel it.

Belinda Sinclair I hadn't seen the stage show before I auditioned for Janet, but I had read the reviews and thought, "How fantastic for Richard that it was doing so well." I couldn't believe how successful the show was. People were queuing up to get in!

Jeffrey Weinstock The original run at the Royal Court Theatre Upstairs generated a lot of attention and praise. It was originally scheduled for just three weeks, but demand was so high that it got extended to five.

Patricia Quinn I wasn't surprised by the success of the play at the Theatre Upstairs. It was amazing. It was all word of mouth. We just became a hit overnight, and it felt normal to me. Sixty people came every night.

The musical was a success from the start. As Rocky would say, it was no way to behave on its first day out, but since it was such an exceptional beauty, we're prepared to forgive it. However, in the weeks after Rocky debuted, the whole of London became obsessed with Tim Curry's performance—and that now-iconic entrance. You know the one.

Karen Tongson When Frank-N-Furter throws off that cloak and reveals himself, revealing his gender-ambiguous cloak to show his femme, fabulous self was shocking. There was no concealing anything. That boldness was truly striking. That was a pretty bold move for a film in the '70s.

Richard Hartley I'll never forget the first time Tim threw off his cloak in the theater. There was this incredible sense of joy in the audience. Some were shocked at first, but then they laughed,

Left: Frank sitting on Eddie's resting place.
Opposite: The floor show, with Belinda Sinclair as Janet

"The nice thing about performing *Rocky* is it's fun to do. You don't come offstage thinking, 'Oh God, it was hard work.' It's just such fun to do because it's silly nonsense. You don't even have to work selling comedy. The comedy will take care of itself."

—Richard O'Brien

completely taken by it. From the very first preview, Tim had this ability to control the crowd—he could switch between sweet and menacing in an instant. That was his magic onstage. He knew exactly how to play the audience.

Tim Curry "Sweet Transvestite" announced my arrival in a way that is difficult to ignore as long as I delivered it with authority.

Richard O'Brien That opening line, "I'm just a sweet transvestite," is powerful because it was so fucking brave and quite shocking. Women in the audience, until that exact moment, had no idea that they would find a creature like Frank that attractive. It was liberating.

Sue Blane With the high collar and Tim's dark curly hair, he could virtually emerge on the scene, which was really important. So we made the cloak so he could bust it all up. And his hands needed to be free for the mic, so the cloak had to be long enough to allow that. It was all very dark. We practiced it lots of times, with him in the cloak, to do the reveal. I can't remember if I used a cord tie, but it slipped open easily.

Tim Curry I had a rather good entrance in the original play because it was a tiny theater. And I came down this sort of wooden staircase and then, when I threw off the cloak, there was a definite frisson, which was good because that was what was meant to happen.

Barry Bostwick When Tim made his entrance and just blows the walls off the Roxy [the Los Angeles theater where the play would eventually run], I knew this was something I had to be part of. I fell in love with the show, and I fell in love with Tim.

Nell Campbell After sashaying down the aisle from the back of the theater, once Tim hits the stage, he just throws off his cape. And there he is in the corset, the garters, the fishnet, the whole goddamn kit and caboodle. Everyone just went nuts. It was incredible.

Jim Sharman One of the unique elements of the original Upstairs production was the ramps surrounding the audience. Tim entered

from behind them—but also among them. I actually asked Brian to adjust the height of the ramps so that when Tim's stilettos stamped down, they would be at eye level with the audience. It created a real sense of physical danger. That added a dynamic quality to his entrance—mysterious and alarming. Of course, once the theaters got bigger, that effect was impossible to reproduce.

Patricia Quinn Tim's legendary entrance was a bit of a necessity. We were in a sixty-seat room, and Brian Thomson, the set designer, put scaffolding everywhere to make the space work. The set was just the width of my hands, and there was only one wooden chair. There wasn't space for the band, so they put a cinema screen up behind the stage to hide the musicians. The set became a bit like a demolition site, and we had scaffolding to climb on.

Tim Curry I had such a ball in that Royal Court theater because I was down in the middle of the audience half the time, on a ramp, which was an extremely vulnerable place to be, but a very authoritative kind of place to be. And it gave me power.

Joel Thurm The only missed opportunity of the movie, I felt, was Tim Curry's entrance. In the theater, he walked down the aisle from the back of the Roxy, and it was incredible. They tried to replicate that with the brass elevator in the movie, but nothing could beat the real thing.

Richard Hartley Tim's entrance in the original stage play, I think, is one of the best entrances in a musical ever. People were just laughing.

Susan Sarandon I had a friend, Jamie Donnelly, who was in the stage show at the Roxy. She played Magenta. I didn't know about *The Rocky Horror Show* until I came to LA. And I got to know Tim when I saw that show. That moment when he entered was and still is one of the most electrifying moments I've ever seen onstage. He came on, and it just blew everyone away.

Five weeks of triumph at the Theatre Upstairs ended with a canceled final night performance on July 26, 1973, that was anything but a happy ending. Blood, sweat, and tears and a swollen, glittery penis became the stars of the show. Just another day in the life of Rocky Horror.

EXIT

Rayner Bourton (Rocky), sporting the infamous glass glitter that brought down the final London performance.

Nell Campbell On the final night of *The Rocky Horror Show* at the Royal Court, summer of 1973, Mick Jagger was in the audience. We were beside ourselves. That was peak Rolling Stones period.

Patricia Quinn In 1973, we were really with it. On our final night of our first run, I remember walking past Mick Jagger and Bianca at the Royal Court. Bianca was in her signature white suit with a cane, and Elliott Gould was with them. I just walked by them nonchalantly and went up the stairs to our dressing room. I thought, "Oh, Jagger's here." But that night, something strange happened.

Rayner Bourton When we were performing the show, I only had one costume change, from the glittery shorts to the finale costume. To help define my shape, I would cover myself in oil and glitter to show the muscle outlines. The glitter was made from powdered glass. We didn't have the same care taken of costumes as there is now, and the outfit was covered in glitter from previous nights' shows. Basically, on the Friday-night show I got glitter where it shouldn't go, and it sliced the end of my penis. I awoke on the Saturday in the most pain I have ever been in my life. The show must go on, as they say, so I tried cold baths and even a cold shower before the show. The pain just got worse. We were meant to start the show at 10:30, and by 8:30 there was one member of the audience already there: Mick Jagger! We had to tell him that the show was canceled as Rocky had something wrong with his cock. Mick's reply was "Well, darling, don't we all." Worse was to come as the doctor decided that the swelling would have to be lanced. I still have the scars.

Richard O'Brien I remember our show on the last night at the Royal Court was canceled, which was a shame. Mick Jagger and Elliott Gould were on the stairs trying to get in, and we had to turn them away. "Why?" they said. "Well, Rocky's got a little bit of glitter in an uncomfortable part of his anatomy." And I'm going, "No, stop it. Oh, come on, for Christ sakes." So I went downstairs, and he's down in the shower. I was about to give him a bit of a "buck up" kind of speech. And a doctor came past us with a bag and stood in front of the shower, and he said, "All right, let's have a . . . Oh my goodness!" And, well, it was a sight to be seen actually. And once seen, never forgotten. And so we didn't go on that night, sadly. But yes, Mick and Elliott Gould got turned away that night.

Almost immediately after it was written, Richard's infectious and interactive "The Time Warp" became the breakout song of the show and an earworm for the ages. In the movie, it introduced the audience to a bunch of Transylvanians and a dance craze that even humans could do. For every generation since 1973, "The Time Warp" has remained a popular classic and shows no signs of aging.

Jim Sharman The breakthrough moment in rehearsals came when Richard walked in and performed "The Time Warp," which I gather he had worked out at home with his then-wife, Kimi. That changed everything. If we're talking about the beginning of a cult, it started with "Time Warp." Richard also did the original choreography, which I suspect he and Kimi had refined, but the idea itself never changed from the start.

Richard O'Brien "The Time Warp" came about during rehearsal. It was inspired by an *Astounding Tales* cover I had on my table. I'm pretty sure it was the exact same edition. I looked at it and thought, "It's astounding." That's when the lyrics came together: "Time is fleeting, madness takes its toll," and then, "But listen closely, not for very much longer." At that point, the song transitions back into dialogue, pushing the story forward and integrating the plot into the lyrics.

Nell Campbell Jim would say, "Can you write a song for the three servants? And they do a little dance together?" Richard went home with his then-wife, Kimi, and invented a dance, then wrote a song to match it. Before rehearsals the next morning in the Theatre

Right: Patricia Quinn (Magenta) and Richard O'Brien (Riff Raff) do "The Time Warp."
Following pages: Final bows of the London cast.

Upstairs, he swung by Richard Hartley's tiny basement flat opposite the Court, and they finessed the chorus. They arrived on time for rehearsal with "The Time Warp." Richard always delivered.

Richard O'Brien "The Time Warp" just sort of wrote itself one evening.

Patricia Quinn Richard came in the next day with the direction: "It's just a jump to the left, and then a step to the right, with your hands on your hips." He showed us the dance, and we've all been doing it ever since. It was the Hokey Cokey—"You put your right foot in, you put your right foot out, and shake it all about"—but better.

Jack Black: The song "Time Warp" grabbed me instantly. It's a powerful jam with a catchy hook. It's the song I wanted to hear again and again. I'd call it the centerpiece of the movie's music masterpiece.

Richard O'Brien The "Time Warp" dance was just silly. I was making fun of all those dance crazes like the Twist, Hucklebuck, and Madison. It was more for comedy than anything else.

"Over the years, the most common question I get asked is, was I shocked when I first read the script? Punk was just happening. I had a very left-liberal upbringing with marvelous parents, so there was absolutely nothing shocking about it. But it's interesting that so many people assumed we would be shocked."

—Nell Campbell

CHAPTER 3

IT'S NOT EASY HAVING A GOOD TIME

It's alive! With *Rocky* now firmly on his feet and the early stagings of the stage show in London a success, it wasn't long before theaters in Los Angeles and New York, and Hollywood movie producers, made the call. Fans no longer need to wait in antici . . . . pation to see the show. It was everywhere—and in abundance!

THEATRE
KING'S
ROAD
THEATRE
THE
ROCKY HORROR
SHOW
BY RICHARD O'BRIEN
THE KINGSROAD THEATRE
ROCKY HORROR THE
SHOW ROCKY HORROR
SHOW

In August 1973, The Rocky Horror Show *transferred from the Royal Court's Theatre Upstairs to Classic Cinema, King's Road, and ran for three months. It moved again to the King's Road Theatre in November 1973 and set up shop for six years and nearly three thousand performances.*

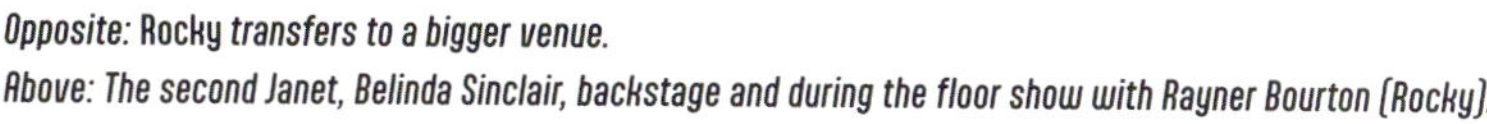

Opposite: Rocky transfers to a bigger venue.
Above: The second Janet, Belinda Sinclair, backstage and during the floor show with Rayner Bourton (Rocky).

Richard O'Brien We originally had a three-week run at the Theatre Upstairs, but we got an extra two weeks. And then Julie Covington left. She went to do *Antony and Cleopatra* with Vanessa Redgrave. We had a three-week break, and then Belinda Sinclair came in to replace her. *Rocky* was fringe theater, and Julie got a bigger job. She didn't realize *Rocky* was going to last for fifty years.

Jim Sharman With every transfer to a new theater, the show evolved in some way.

Nell Campbell After Julie Covington left the show, Belinda Sinclair took over and was fabulous as Janet.

Belinda Sinclair In August 1973, I suddenly got a call from Richard saying the show he had written was going to be put on. He asked me if I wanted to meet Jim Sharman and audition for a role. I said, "Of course!" Elaine Paige was auditioning with me, but luckily I got the part. I sang my standard song, "Every Time We Say Goodbye."

Richard O'Brien Belinda Sinclair sang the songs on the original cast soundtrack album [released in late 1973] before she had even performed the show live.

Belinda Sinclair After I got the part, I saw the show before it left the Royal Court. I knew what it was about and how it came about. During rehearsals, I added a few things, like the line "Didn't we pass a castle?" And I definitely invented the windscreen wiper. They have a car onstage now, but we never had one, so I became the windscreen wiper.

I tried to make Janet a real person, not just a character. I didn't base her on anyone I knew or any specific characters. I just tried to embody her as a real person. I didn't try to copy Julie's version—

"*Rocky* has nothing to do with shocking people. I wrote *Rocky* for me. I didn't write it with an audience in mind or for it to be a hit."

—Richard O'Brien

I couldn't possibly have copied her voice. She had the most wonderful voice.

Patricia Quinn There was a lot of discussion about what theater it could go to next. We ended up at the Chelsea Classic. It was about to be demolished, so the scaffolding on the outside worked perfectly. After that, I left.

Belinda Sinclair When I joined, the production felt like one big party. At first, I didn't take it too seriously. It was just fun. We were all half naked most of the time, but it was fine because everyone was so loving and thrilled by the show's success.

Nell Campbell I was in the show for seven months, from the Upstairs theater to the King's Road and then to the sold-out Chelsea Classic. Jim and Brian Thomson didn't want the show to go into the West End—it was far too conventional for them. After seven months, I felt I couldn't do "The Time Warp" again. Tim was leaving to do the show in Los Angeles, and other original cast members had already left for bigger roles and more money. I left to go busking in the South of France. Yep, I left the most successful show in London to go busking in the South of France!

Belinda Sinclair I first met Tim Curry on the first day of rehearsals in August 1973. I remember him being shy and nervous. When I saw him as Frank, he completely transformed. He was no longer Tim. It was mind-blowing. I continued to be amazed by him every night for four years and got to do a sex scene with him every night behind the screen. It was wonderful. I loved him as a person, and he was incredibly sexy. Both men and women loved him and were deeply attracted to him.

Richard O'Brien By the time we got to the King's Road Theatre, a five hundred–seater, we had a catwalk down the middle of the auditorium. The noise started behind the audience—this "boom doom doom doom" sound—and this creature, Frank, walked down the aisle. He was wearing ripped fishnet stockings, with bruises on his legs, blood streaking down, and plasters from where he'd shot up. The audience, which was a pretty average crowd for a fringe theater show, was taken aback. They had no idea they'd find Frank so attractive, but they did. When he turned and gave that smile, it was like a switch flipped, and they surprised themselves by their attraction to this character. It was quite extraordinary.

Belinda Sinclair After the Theatre Upstairs, we moved to a club called the Pheasantry on King's Road first, but it didn't feel quite right. Then we moved to the Classic, further down the road, and that's where the show really exploded.

Nell Campbell We moved the show to the Chelsea Classic theater after five weeks at Royal Court. The Classic was set to be demolished in three months. My pay went up to £50 a week. I felt rich! I had been squatting and getting by on £18 a week, so £50 was a fortune.

Belinda Sinclair "Touch Me" was my favorite song to sing because I sang half of it upside down, with my legs around Rocky's waist, then fell back and finished the song.

Richard O'Brien When we transferred to the Classic Cinema in Chelsea, I came out of the first night, and Michael White, our producer, said: "I think we've got a hit, Richard!" And I said: "Have we?" Tennessee Williams came to see the show on our first night at the Classic theater. Afterwards, as I was heading to my dressing room, I heard, "Tennessee Williams wants to meet the author." I thought, "Oh my God, that's me!" I quickly changed and walked up to him. He was sitting in the audience and had either had too much medication or not enough. I nervously introduced myself, saying, "Mr. Williams, it's such a pleasure. I adore your work." He responded with something I couldn't quite catch. His companion translated, saying, "He loves your work too."

Nell Campbell How many people I slept with in the cast. Sadly, I can't tell you. I'm just going to let that sit there.

Richard O'Brien The nice thing about the first performances was there was no pressure on us. We were just having fun. Things going wrong was part of it. Even when we transferred to King's Road, we were free. There was nobody looking to turn it into what it's become.

Jim Sharman Richard and I talked at this time about how the show had become this quasi-punk phenomenon. I asked him, "Is this how you imagined it?" He said, "No. I imagined it as a kind of midrange musical."

Opposite and above: Alive on stage! A newspaper ad for King's Road, and a poster for the Classic. Following pages: Dr. Scott (Paddy O'Hagan) and Brad (Christopher Malcolm) aren't having as much fun as Frank (Tim Curry) is.

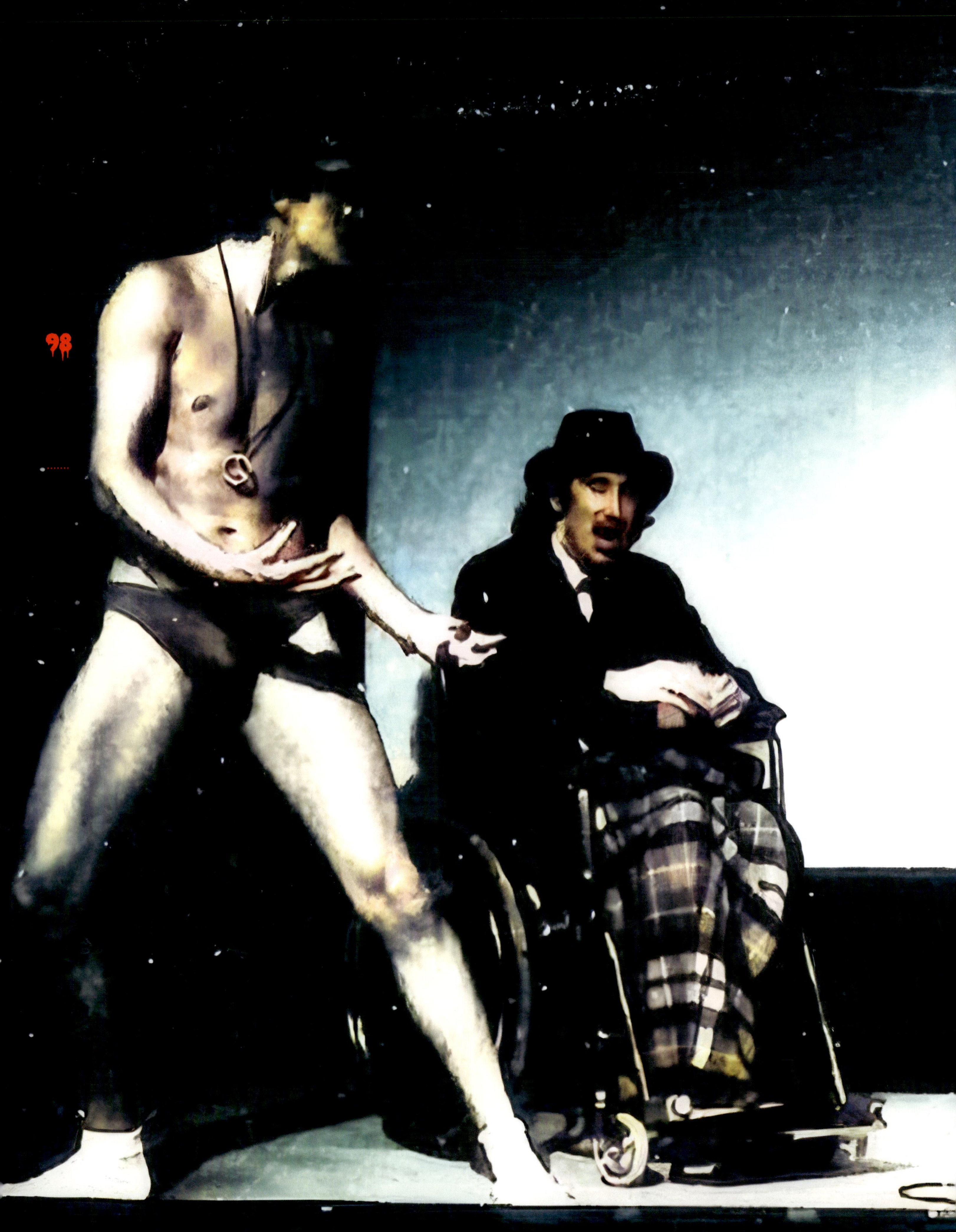

Richard O'Brien and Tim Curry at the Evening Standard Theatre Awards.

"Everybody wanted to be in the movie, but no one wanted to do the stage show in LA."

—Joel Thurm

Richard O'Brien In January 1973, the Evening Standard Award voted *Rocky* Best Musical 1973—fantastic! It was the equal of having an Emmy. It was the big one to get. I went to the ceremony. It was rather lovely, because I was standing there, and Laurence Olivier made a speech, saying, "This is the most wonderful award I've ever had in my entire life." After he came off the stage and I was standing there, he walked straight up to me and shook my hand.

With the dawn rising on 1974, Tim Curry left the original London cast behind to perform the show in a new production at the Roxy Theatre, Los Angeles, alongside American actors in the remaining roles. Opening night was March 19, 1974. Among those in attendance for the premiere were John Lennon, Mick and Bianca Jagger, Roman Polanski, Jack Nicholson, Anjelica Huston, and Cher.

Producer Lou Adler with Britt Ekland.

Richard O'Brien When the show became a success and we were taking Tim to Los Angeles, we had another round of auditions for the London show at the King's Road Theatre. The cattle call was on Tuesday mornings, and a crowd of people turned up. I decided to bring several bottles of wine—both red and white—and offer them to the auditionees. One guy came in and said, "I don't care whether I get the part or not, but this is the most wonderful, wonderful audition opening ever!" It was a small gesture, but it felt like decency, and it made the experience even more memorable.

Lou Adler I first saw *The Rocky Horror Show* in 1973, thanks to Britt Ekland, a Swedish-English movie star and my girlfriend at the time. One day, Britt mentioned a musical called *Rocky Horror Show*, which was all the rage in London. I flew to London and, jet-lagged, went to see it. I immediately fell for the show. That night, at a party, I met Michael White, the original producer of *The Rocky Horror Show*. He knew who I was and made a deal for me to handle the American distribution of the play.

Jim Sharman Britt Ekland was the one who led Lou Adler to *Rocky Horror*. She told him he had to see it. I'd venture to say Lou, being a sharp producer, may have already been thinking ahead—that staging it at the Roxy could be a step toward a film.

Lou Adler My business partner, Elmer Valentine, had opened the Whisky a Go Go on Sunset Boulevard. He told me the Largo, a burlesque house on Sunset, might be available for purchase. We decided to buy it and open a new club—the Roxy—in September 1973.

Joel Thurm Lou Adler asked me to cast a stage production of *Rocky* in the US at Lou's LA. brand-new nightclub, the Roxy. I had friends in London who had told me all about the show. They said it was wonderful, so I was already aware of it when Lou Adler offered me the job to cast it in LA.

Lou Adler I had two ideas in mind. First, I wanted to put it in the Roxy because of how it was presented in London. The Roxy was perfect for it—a cabaret-style setting where you could go beyond just sitting in a theater and fully immerse yourself in the experience. And in the back of my mind, I envisioned it as a film from the very beginning.

Coca-Cola
ACME

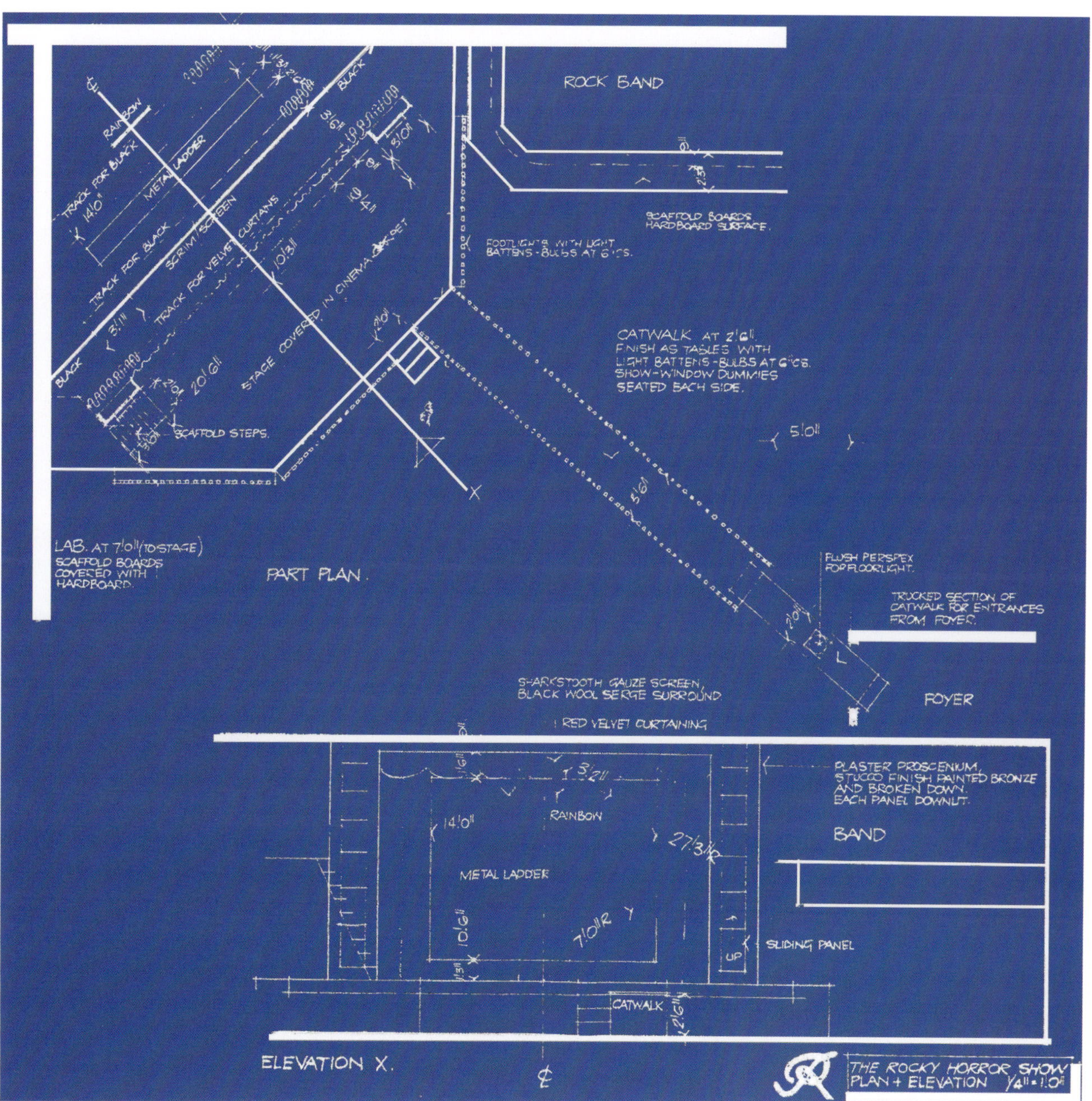

Opposite: The interior of the Roxy.
Above: The blueprints for the stage setup.

Jim Sharman One of the biggest choices I made—both for better and worse—was in casting. Traditionally, musicals run on Broadway, and a decade later, Hollywood makes a film version with an entirely new cast. We broke every rule. Lou Adler [the film's producer] set up the film after producing the *Rocky Horror* stage show at the Roxy in LA, where film industry people could come see it.

Joel Thurm Sometimes casting can be harder than rocket science. But *Rocky Horror* in LA wasn't. Tim was an indispensable part of it. The main challenge in casting for the Roxy was that agents and anyone I called didn't know about it. If they did, they would read the script and reject it, often referring to it as trash or garbage—and those were the nicer comments.

Jim Sharman knew who Barry Bostwick was and, most importantly, recognized his talent. The minute I got the job to cast the Roxy production, I wanted Barry Bostwick for Brad. But he turned me down.

Barry Bostwick I first heard about *Rocky* through Joel Thurm, the casting director. He asked me if I would be interested in coming to LA and doing the production at the Roxy. I told him I didn't really want to do a stage play at that point. But if there was ever going to be a movie, please come to me and talk to me about playing a character in it.

Tim Curry Lou Adler knew how to put on a show. He had searchlights outside the theater in the sky, and it was a big deal, the opening night. It was a tad overwhelming, really.

Lou Adler Opening night at the Roxy was something truly special. It wasn't just about the old celebrities, but about the new rock and roll icons like John Lennon. Most celebrities wanted to be there because they were aware of what had happened in London—either having seen it in person or knowing about it. It felt like a throwback to the '40s—those kinds of events, the openings, and the way people dressed. It was really very special.

Tim Curry I do remember the opening night at the Roxy, because I remember I was in the box office in my costume, all ready to go on. That's where I was kind of corralled. And so I was aware of people going past into the hallway that led into the theater. And I remember Mick and Bianca Jagger coming in and Bianca saying, "We cannot go on going out like this."

Jeffrey Weinstock Keith Moon, the drummer for the Who, was apparently a massive *Rocky Horror* fan. He attended regularly shows at the Roxy and afterwards would leave nine bottles of champagne on the front of the stage—one for each cast member.

John Lennon attends Rocky Horror's *opening night at the Roxy.*

Once Lou Adler's LA production of Rocky *was up and running at the Roxy, a veritable buffet of soon-to-be-famous faces auditioned to be part of the all-new cast. Including one Mr. Loaf. But you can call him Meat.*

The no-good kid: Meat Loaf as Eddie.

Meat Loaf My background with theater started when I was a sophomore in high school in drama and musicals. In college I took constitutional law, history, drama, speech therapy, improv, music appreciation—that class I got thrown out of.

Jim Sharman I was in New York around this tim, talking with Jim Steinman—a radical talent who later became a good friend. He had written a musical called *The Dream Engine*, a very radical take on Peter Pan. It never got staged because the J. M. Barrie rights were controlled by a children's hospital in London, and they weren't going to approve his version. That show evolved into *Bat Out of Hell*. Through Steinman, I connected with Meat Loaf. He had this massive voice—the sound of the '80s before the '80s even arrived. In the LA production, he played both Eddie and Dr. Scott. Richard O'Brien saw him and knew immediately—that was our Eddie.

Joel Thurm By the time I joined in 1974, the most difficult role was already cast—Tim Curry's role. The next tough one was Eddie. However, Meat Loaf just walked into an audition, and that was it. He had an incredible voice.

Jeffrey Weinstock Meat Loaf had spent years trying to break into the music industry, fronting several bands that didn't take off. He eventually turned to theater and landed a role in a touring production of *Hair*. That's where Richard O'Brien first saw him. Meat Loaf was then invited to audition for Eddie in the Roxy production of *Rocky Horror*—and got the part.

Meat Loaf Richard and Jim came to me for the part of "Hot Patootie," and Richard O'Brien is here at these rehearsals . . . He said, "On this song, you'll never be able to get all the words in. I wrote it, and I can't sing all the words." I looked at him and said, "I can sing all the words." I just love telling people "I can do that" and then being able to do it.

Richard Hartley Meat Loaf completely rephrased "Hot Patootie," especially the verses. We just gave Meat Loaf space to work. He broke the microphone with his powerful voice when he recorded the song—this very expensive mic with a tiny diaphragm. It cracked! I just said, "Get another one." I remember after we recorded it, I got a call from the producer Lou Adler saying that

Opposite: Eddie (Meat Loaf) makes his entrance in the original Roxy cast production, c. 1974. Following pages: Dr. Scott (Meat Loaf) living his life for the thrills in the floor show.

Meat Loaf wasn't happy with his performance. So he came back and rerecorded some sections.

Patricia Quinn Meat Loaf was amazing. I'll never forget the first time I met him. We were rehearsing [for the movie], and I walked in to see this guy—a redneck Texan, I thought. Who is he? He was new to me, though he'd done the show in LA and had come from that. Then he sang. In that empty hotel room with a chandelier, I swear it shook. It reminded me of when I was a girl watching Caruso with my mother—when he sang, everything trembled. Meat Loaf's voice was just as astonishing. Later, on set, he came up to me and said, "I was voted the best kisser in my high school in Texas." "Oh, really?" I said. "Well, let's see." So we kissed. And I had to admit, they were right—he was the best kisser in his high school.

Lou Adler Meat Loaf was almost the opposite of Tim—rock with a touch of theater, and that impressed me. His size and his name were part of what made him special. For the Roxy, we had some incredibly talented people, most of whom were local actors.

Jeffrey Weinstock Meat Loaf once talked about his first introduction to *Rocky* when he joined the LA cast at the Roxy. Jim Sharman had withheld the script from new cast members, so they didn't really know what they were getting into. According to Meat Loaf, when Tim Curry performed "Sweet Transvestite," that was the moment he said, "Nope," and he walked out. He claimed he wasn't going to do a "transvestite show." Clearly, he came around, but I think that reaction gives some indication of just how shocking Frank-N-Furter's reveal must have been in 1974/'75—seeing him in full transvestite regalia for the first time.

Nell Campbell I saw Meat Loaf play Eddie and Dr. Scott at a show in LA before he was cast in the movie. He was an unknown—just a singer and actor, not famous yet. We referred to him as Mr. Loaf.

Barry Bostwick Meat Loaf and I had been New York actors and auditioned against each other many times for roles on Broadway. I knew him a little bit.

Joel Thurm One night at the Roxy, Meat Loaf almost died because the Coke machine he was inside before he made his stage entrance ran out of air . . . and he couldn't get out!

"Elvis Presley came to see the stage version of *The Rocky Horror Picture Show* at the Roxy. He asked to see me and Tim Curry after the show. That meeting happened in the private room over the Rainbow Bar. He wanted to meet me and Tim. I walked right up to him, and he asked me a question, and all I did was shake my head. He asked, 'I hear that everybody else had been impersonating me when they did the character of Eddie, but you didn't.' I did answer that because that was an actor question, so I was capable of answering that one. I said, 'There's no point in me imitating you because it would be impossible.' That's all I said to him."

—Meat Loaf

Contenders for Dr. Frank-N-Furter's Throne: Mick Jagger, David Bowie, and Lou Reed.

With the Broadway production at the Belasco opening its doors in March 1975, and the show still a hit in LA and London, the Rocky creators in summer 1974 began their next side hustle: preproduction for The Rocky Horror Picture Show. *For Richard, Tim, Jim, and the rest of the original cast (plus some new faces), it was time to do "The Time Warp" all over again.*

Richard O'Brien During the stage run at the Roxy in LA, there were talks about making a movie. Mick Jagger's company wanted to buy the film rights. I met with his team, then told Jim, "Jagger's people want to buy the rights." He said, "Don't do it." I asked why, and he explained, "If they buy it, we won't be able to do it." So I backed off.

Patricia Quinn David Bowie came to the show in King's Road. He wanted to play Frank. Mick Jagger too. They all wanted to play Frank for the film. But Jim Sharman refused any big star names. No Mick Jagger, no Bowie. He said, "I'm having the original cast, thank you." [The film studio] 20th Century Fox even tried to cancel it when they realized Jim wouldn't employ any stars.

Barry Bostwick Every actor in the world wanted to be Frank-N-Furter because of the depth of that character and the flamboyance—and the meanness of him.

Lou Adler I don't know if Mick would have ever seriously played Frank. I would have liked to have seen him do the narrator role, though. Tim Curry's look in the movie must have had some influence on David Bowie and Mick and a lot of artists at that time.

Nell Campbell Three megastars wanted to play roles in the movie—Mick Jagger, Lou Reed, and, of course, David Bowie. Jim now says that had he used any famous people, let alone them, there would be no cult.

Tim Curry It was smart of Jim Sharman to keep the original cast. I'm glad he did. Certainly Patricia Quinn, who played Magenta, was totally splendid in the movie. And it's very easy to caricature a part like that, which she never did. She was also astonishingly beautiful.

Jim Sharman I expected to be asked to direct the movie. What surprised me at first was that only I was being asked—initially, none of the original cast. But I felt a deep sense of commitment to the people who had created it with me.

Richard O'Brien Halfway through 1974, we got the news that the movie would be made, with Jim directing and Tim playing the lead. Then Alan Ladd Jr. took over as head of 20th Century Fox [the film's financier and distributor]. As often happens, a new head wants to push out any projects left on the desk. Despite his reluctance, we were too far along to cancel. He came to the set with four angry men, as I recall. Bad-tempered men walking around, shuffling and huffling and unhappy. None of them wanted to make *Rocky*.

John Goldstone Michael White was a really interesting theater producer. He did groundbreaking shows. He was a risk-taker, and he could spot something original, which I guess is how he came to *Rocky Horror Show*. I met Michael in 1968, and I'd had some experience in film production that he did not have. We formed a company together to produce films. In '73, we produced Monty Python's *Holy Grail,* so by '74, when Richard O'Brien and Jim Sharman had written a script based on their live show, Michael and I wanted to see how we could make a film of that.

I saw the original stage production when it moved to the King's Road. It was sold out. The show could be done as a film. It was just a question of how.

Richard O'Brien When someone suggested we do *Rocky* as a film, I just went along for the ride. I said, "Oh yeah, sure." I was very casual about the whole thing. It seemed quite surreal to me. I never went home and said, "Wow! We're going to make a movie!" I've thought about it since, though, and said, "Wow! We made a movie!"

John Goldstone I made a deal with Michael [White] to bring the stage show to America. Lou [Adler] obviously had to know what the film was going to cost before he could go to Fox, so the three of us put together a believable budget. Even then, it was a very risky project to finance.

Jim Sharman There's a bit of a myth that the studio insisted we cast Americans as Brad and Janet. That actually seemed logical to me—real Americans playing real Americans. But I was determined to keep the core family together: Frank, Riff Raff, Magenta, and Columbia.

No transmit bean for Brad and Janet: Christopher Malcolm and Belinda Sinclair were the only London cast members not brought on for the movie.

Belinda Sinclair I was very disappointed not to be in the movie. So was Chris Malcolm. Jim Sharman really wanted me to be part of it, but he didn't have a choice. I understood—of course, we were meant to be the all-American couple, but you can't have an English woman and a Canadian guy playing that role. The distributors wouldn't have accepted it. But it was incredibly disappointing.

Richard O'Brien I would have thought that our original Brad, Chris Malcolm, wasn't particularly happy about being recast. But I think it was the right thing to do.

The movie's Janet and Brad: Susan Sarandon and Barry Bostwick.

"One of the best things about the play's success was that we, as a fringe theater, were allowed to make a movie, with Jim directing, Brian Thomson as the artistic director, and Tim in the lead role—rare for Hollywood, where they'd usually recast for a bigger name."

—Richard O'Brien

John Goldstone Recasting the two British leads of Brad and Janet—Chris Malcolm and Belinda Sinclair—we felt it was good to have two real Hollywood actors playing those parts. And they were the right choice. Both Susan [Sarandon] and Barry [Bostwick] have spoken about how being newcomers to this group of people who were already somewhat unified kind of mirrored their own characters. Strangers in a strange land, and all that.

Lou Adler It was hard to argue against keeping the original cast actors, as they weren't just actors—they had created those parts and characters. I don't recall it being much of a fight with Fox. The fight was to add Americans to it, and we ended up with two perfect replacements—Susan Sarandon and Barry Bostwick.

Nell Campbell At first, we resented bitterly Susan and Barry being thrust upon us as Brad and Janet, because we wanted our original Brad and Janet—Belinda Sinclair and Chris Malcolm. In my mind, it should have been Belinda and Chris Malcolm in the film. It was disappointing when they weren't.

Richard O'Brien One of the nicest things about the movie casting process was that during the rehearsal period, Susan Sarandon and Barry Bostwick came over from America and stepped into a world (that we already inhabited). It was exactly how it was meant to be and felt completely natural. Rehearsing was a dream because we all knew our roles, and they came in like the "virgins," fitting perfectly into the world we had already created.

Barry Bostwick I had seen the play before I was cast. I saw Tim do it at the Roxy, and it blew me away!

Susan Sarandon I had no intentions of having anything to do with the movie, as I don't sing. But I went with Barry to his audition just to say hi, and they were like "Why don't you read Janet?" Janet at that time felt to me like a satire of every ingenue I'd ever played, you know, somebody who's kind of wide-eyed and sweet. But underneath is a bitch. I read it, and I thought that was fun.

Richard Hartley said, "Everyone that had played Janet before were really singers." And I said, "Well, I can't really sing." And I'd always had a phobia about singing in public. My dad was a singer, was a band singer before the war. And I was always told I couldn't sing and to be quiet and everything. "Oh, come on, everybody can sing," Jim and Richard said. "Just sing 'Happy Birthday.'" And so I did. And then they offered me the part, and I thought, "It's such an ego trip to be so self-involved that you're afraid to sing 'Happy Birthday.' Just get over it, girl." And then I told my agent I wanted to be in the film.

Barry Bostwick When the movie became a reality, Joel Thurm had me come in for a meet and greet because I don't think everybody knew who I was. I didn't have to do an audition, apparently. But Joel was very sneaky because Susan Sarandon, who was a friend of mine at the time, he was interested in her to play Janet, but her agent apparently didn't want her to audition.

Joel Thurm Susan's agents, CMA, didn't want her to audition. They didn't object to her being in the film, but they wouldn't let her audition. I knew Jim and Richard needed her to, so when Barry came in for his audition, I told him to bring Susan, and I'd handle the rest. [During the audition] I was reading with Barry when I stopped and said, "Why am I, a thirty-year-old balding man, reading with you when we have a lovely woman here? Susan, could you do me a favor and read with Barry?" She wasn't auditioning; she was just there. As soon as Susan started reading, Jim turned to me and asked, "Who is she?"

Barry Bostwick When we arrived, I thought the focus was going to be on me, but apparently who they were really looking at was Susan! I already had the job—but I didn't know it—and Joel was just sort of suckering me in!

Joel Thurm As Susan read with Barry, Jim asked me, "Can she sing?" I said, "I don't know. Let's ask her." She sang "Happy Birthday," and it was a sweet soprano voice. Susan didn't need to be a great singer. We could've found someone more technically skilled, but Susan brought something else.

Barry Bostwick Susan and I were both cast on the day from that meet and greet with everybody. I don't even know if I ever read a script.

Barry Bostwick When Susan and I showed up in London for the two-week rehearsal and then the filming, we were outliers. We were people out of everybody's focus. And I think it's good for the film, because we were strangers in a strange land—a very strange land.

Richard Hartley Susan Sarandon was perfect for the role—warm, not too aggressive, and just right. Julie Covington was a bit more aggressive onstage. Some actresses today, especially in theatrical productions, copy Susan Sarandon's approach. She's beautiful, warm, and playful.

Joel Thurm The biggest change going from stage to screen was casting a new Janet. It's a showy part. Thankfully, Susan Sarandon knows how to shine.

Richard O'Brien When you think about Susan's stellar career since then, it was very nice to be part of her springboard.

Above: The billboard in Times Square for the short-lived Belasco run.
Opposite: The poster announcing the New York production.

Oh, I just love success! The nine-month run at the Roxy was a sellout (in a good way), with praise heaped upon Tim Curry and the rest of the cast, including Meat Loaf, Jamie Donnelly, Boni Enten, Abigale Haness, Alan Martin, Kim Milford, Bill Miller, Susan Morse, John Mark Robinson, Bruce Scott, and Graham Jarvis. A transfer to New York's Broadway was all but inevitable. On March 10, 1975, the show started its run at the Belasco Theatre. You could say it had a, er, rocky start . . . and end.

Jeffrey Weinstock The Broadway production at the Belasco Theatre was a complete disaster. It got terrible reviews and closed after just forty-five performances. The biggest issue? *Rocky Horror* thrived in its original form as a low-budget, campy, underground experience. When they tried to translate it into a slick, polished Broadway production, it lost a lot of what made it special.

Richard O'Brien After filming, we opened at the Belasco on Broadway in early '75, but it was short-lived. Lou Adler's idea was to replicate the Roxy vibe with tables and chairs for people to drink, but the layout didn't work for a Broadway theater. Unlike the Roxy, where the open layout was effective, a theater demands that the audience faces the stage. With tables placed differently, it led to discomfort, and ultimately it didn't succeed.

Lou Adler I wanted the play to go to New York, to Broadway, but it had to be in a very special situation. The perfect opportunity came about when I found a venue forty minutes from Broadway. It was a place that resembled the old Cocoanut Grove in LA, one of those grand, classic theaters with orchestras and live performers. It mainly hosted weddings and bar mitzvahs, and we had a specific opening date to accommodate the cast. However, the venue owner refused to cancel a bar mitzvah, which forced us to look for another location. My attempt to transform the Belasco Theatre into a Roxy-style cabaret didn't exactly align with the critics' views on the production.

Richard O'Brien There was a snobbery between New York and Los Angeles. LA was seen as flashy, cheap, and tacky, while New York held more prestige. When we came to Broadway, it felt like New York was dismissing us. They didn't like being told *Rocky* was a hit from London and LA Their response was essentially, "We'll decide if it's a hit or not." It was a shame, and the timing, combined with the poor layout and auditorium, worked against us in New York.

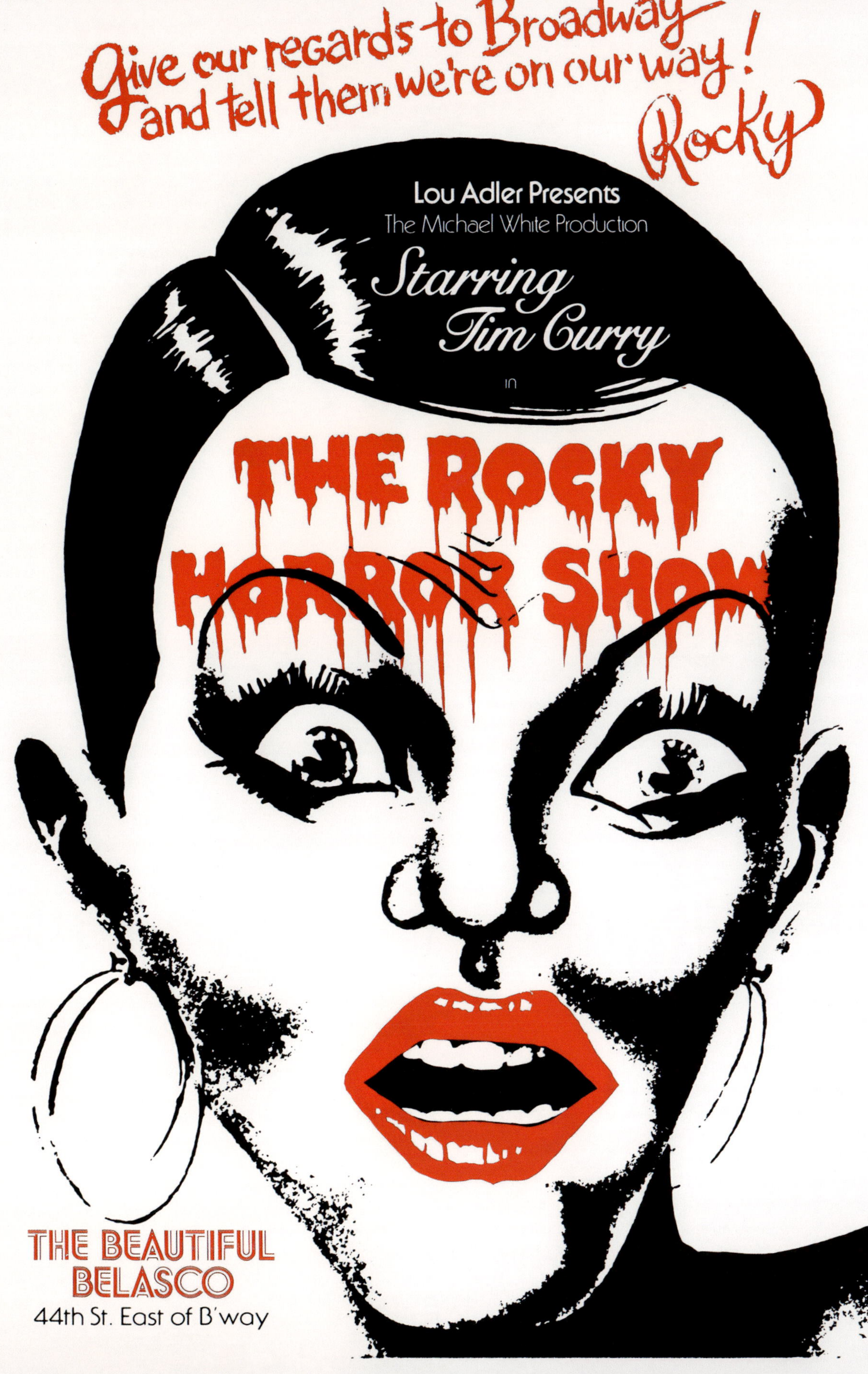
Give our regards to Broadway and tell them we're on our way!
Rocky
Lou Adler Presents
The Michael White Production
Starring
Tim Curry
in
THE ROCKY HORROR SHOW
THE BEAUTIFUL BELASCO
44th St. East of B'way

Above: Rocky (Kim Milford) tried to build up his shoulders, chest, arms, and legs while Frank (Tim Curry) sings of his seven-day plan. Opposite: Promotional photo for the Roxy production. Following pages: Rocky at the start of his pretty big downer.

Richard Hartley Jim knew that making a Broadway version of *The Rocky Horror Show* wasn't a good idea—it just wasn't a fit.

Richard O'Brien The only negativity I encountered toward the show came during our New York opening. Rex Reed, a vocal critic, dismissed it as "just for homosexuals." This struck me as odd, especially since I suspect Rex himself might have been playing for the other side. The next morning, I was on a radio program with Tim, and they asked how I felt about Rex's review. I replied, "Well, it upset both my wife and my boyfriend."

Lou Adler Coming from the Roxy in LA worked against us too—anything from LA was considered unfit for Broadway. I had taken out a full-page ad in *Billboard* that said, "Give our regards to Broadway, and tell them that *Rocky* is on its way!" They absolutely hated it. They hated me for going that route. We didn't have a great chance going in. I think we ran for about forty days. We got closed the first night after the reviews came out, and at that point, there was no way to overcome those reviews. So, around the forty-fifth day, in the middle of the night, I transformed the cabaret back into a theater, repainted the outside, and we'd go on with the show in the morning.

Richard O'Brien After we closed in New York, I remember standing on Forty-Fourth Street, outside my hotel. Tim was staying at the Algonquin, and I was across the street at the Royalton. I said, "Well, I guess that's it. Three years of a great ride, right?" Tim agreed, "Yep, absolutely. It's been a great ride." And that was it. We all agreed—those three years had been fantastic.

"I was a bit bereft when Broadway all came to an end, because there was nowhere to go in the evening. After three years of being Frank, and finishing on Broadway, it was like somebody had let all the air out of a balloon. It sucked all the energy out of me. My time with Frank was at an end."

—Tim Curry

CHAPTER 4

PREPARE THE TRANSMIT BEAM

As London's best musical of 1973 had now exceeded its master's expectations, it didn't take long for Hollywood to muscle in on the action. *The Rocky Horror Picture Show*—a movie musical based on a musical inspired by movies and musicals—was either going to be a phenomenal flop or a sensational success. In true *Rocky* style, of course, it turned out to be both. And a whole lot more to boot.

As the summer sun set on the year 1974, Jim Sharman began his epic quest to direct the hell out of The Rocky Horror Picture Show. *Before he left on this manic misadventure, he first had to find financing, prepare an inexperienced cast for shooting, find the perfect spooky castle, and write the screenplay with Richard. It's not easy having a good time.*

Nell Campbell Jim Sharman cowrote *The Rocky Horror Picture Show* script with Richard in three weeks over the summer of 1974.

Richard O'Brien I found my job writing the screenplay was a bit like creative secretary. We had the layout, and turning it into a movie is really the job of the director.

Patricia Quinn I could never have imagined the stage show expanding from that little sixty-seat room with just a plank to work on . . . into a movie.

Jim Sharman I was offered two versions of the movie: a low-budget B-movie that allowed me to keep the original Royal Court cast, or a bigger-budget film if I cast rock stars instead. I chose the B-movie route. That decision had consequences—when the film opened, no one knew the cast, so it flopped at first. But later, because the audience wasn't familiar with them, they could adopt them. They could dress up as them. They could become them. In the end, that decision may have killed the film's initial box office, but it also created the cult following.

Patricia Quinn With news of the movie spreading, Richard, Jim, and Tim invited me to lunch at the Ark restaurant in Kensington. They told me they were making a film, something they simply called "The Film." They mentioned that the usherette opening in the stage show wouldn't work in the movie. "So, I'm just playing Magenta?" I said. "Yes." "Oh," I said. Then I added, "I'm not singing 'Science Fiction'?" "No," they confirmed. "Then I'm not doing your film," I said. Richard looked at me and said, "Let's go to John Goldstone's house—he lives just around the corner. We want to show you the sets and

Opposite: Richard O'Brien and director Jim Sharman take a break during the filming of Riff Raff's takeover. Above: Getting the gang back together: the original London cast on the movie set.

"*Rocky* is a parody of the cinema for the stage, so actually putting it on film was a bit disorienting. Were we reverting to the original, the thing that was being parodied? Or was it a comment upon a comment upon a comment?"

—Richard O'Brien

Opposite: Tim, Nell, and Patricia. Above: Richard O'Brien with producers Michael White (center) and Lou Adler (right) on the Rocky *set.*

costumes." So, I went. They showed me the set—a pink laboratory, something called Transylvanian Sun Motorbikes, and costumes I didn't even recognize. I said, "Oh, I'm doing this." That was it.

Jim Sharman From the start, I saw the *Rocky* movie as a dark fairy tale, even more so than the stage version. People overlook how dark *Rocky Horror* actually is. It's wrapped up in fairy floss and fountains, but underneath, there's something else going on.

John Goldstone Often, in filmmaking, if you start with a script that's not good enough, you come out with a film which is even worse. For us, we were starting from a strong stage show that had a good story to tell in a very original way.

Lou Adler I don't think Richard or Jim Sharman, or any of us, realized what kind of film we were making in the beginning. We were making a film for an audience, but we didn't know how big that audience could be, or that they would want to participate so actively. But the film was perfect for that.

Barry Bostwick The rehearsal process for the movie was very fast—and very cold. I loved every minute of it because I was a theater rat. I love rehearsing because I would keep trying different things each time we would do it. Jim Sharman, who was so brilliant, would always lead me back into the direction of reality.

Susan Sarandon I don't remember rehearsing much at all. I think the preparation was mostly about wardrobe, and we talked a little about makeup and hair. As for the singing, all the original cast could have done it in their sleep, since they'd rehearsed it so much. There wasn't a lot of sitting around doing readings of the script.

Karen Tongson The movie is an homage to many different cinematic eras and genres, ranging from the 1930s through the 1950s. It draws from sci-fi classics like *Flash Gordon* (1930s) and *The Day the Earth Stood Still* (1950s), as well as other B films from the '50s and '60s. I see elements of *Metropolis* (1920s) in it too. There are also influences from the *King Kong* narrative—particularly the idea of a monster you grow to love, perhaps even developing Stockholm syndrome.

Opposite: Rocky (Peter Hinwood) emerges, to the delight of his creator (Tim Curry). Above: Director Jim Sharman talks through the "Sword of Damocles" number with Peter Hinwood, while Tim waits with antici . . . .

Top: Michael Rennie in The Day The Earth Stood Still *(1951). Bottom: Director Jim Sharman talks through a scene with Susan and Barry.*

Richard O'Brien One of the best science fiction films ever made, and main inspiration behind *Rocky*'s B-movie homage, is *The Day the Earth Stood Still*. It's beautifully shot, with incredible lighting and cinematography that deserved an Oscar. The black-and-white film is well cast, with Michael Rennie delivering a measured, serious performance—far from being jokey. It carries a profound message and is, in many ways, a wonderful film. My favorite bit of *Rocky Horror* is the reference to *The Day the Earth Stood Still*. The opening lyrics, and the very last thing said in the movie—"And crawling on the planet's face/some insects called the human race/lost in time and lost in space/and meaning"—fit perfectly with the tone of *Rocky*, connecting them in a way that complements the film's themes.

Lou Adler Gordon Stulberg, my attorney at the time, had just become the head of 20th Century Fox. This connection gave me a real opportunity to make a deal—and quick. However, I still had to prove to Gordon that this was a viable project. It was so different at the time. It was a musical, which was unusual to bring back to film. When Gordon moved to Fox, the show had been at the Roxy for about six months. I invited Gordon to the show, but I warned him that if he came, he'd need to bring his kids—he had one child who was fourteen and another who was sixteen. I hoped their excitement would elevate his and help spark the excitement needed to push Gordon Stulberg in the right direction to make the deal.

Jeffrey Weinstock After the contracts for the film were drawn up, Richard O'Brien wanted to take them home overnight to review them carefully. But Lou Adler and Michael White really pushed him to hurry up and sign them right away. As a result, O'Brien was essentially sidelined when it came to receiving proceeds from the film.

John Goldstone With the deal done, we set up the production office in my house in Kensington in the basement. Brian Thomson [the set designer] lived on the street next door. He brought the drawings of the sets around to my house. Peter Beale, Fox's representative, came too. Peter was looking after their interest and wanted to

Michael White attends the Rocky Horror Tribute Show at the Royal Court Theatre, 2006.

"Before Michael White passed, I had lunch with him. He said, 'You do understand, Richard, that we ripped you off, don't you?' I replied, 'Michael, if that penny hadn't dropped by now, that would make me even more foolish.' He apologized for his part in it, and I thanked him—it was very kind of him."

—Richard O'Brien

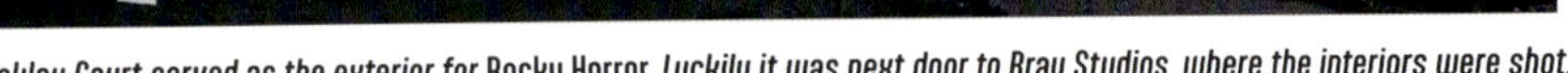

Oakley Court served as the exterior for Rocky Horror. *Luckily it was next door to Bray Studios, where the interiors were shot.*

be sure that we could really do it for the money. I remember he showed us these Ralph McQuarrie drawings for *Star Wars*, which was in very early production for Fox at Pinewood Studios, London. Nobody at Fox understood what that was about, either!

Everyone who worked on the film were all the same age. We'd come out of World War II together, which was a time of great austerity. All our parents were careful about money, and we were part of the Rolling Stones/Beatles generation who were fighting against all of that. The *Rocky* movie came out of that generation of people who wanted to do something very different, and there was certainly an audience to understand the outrage.

Lou Adler As the film's budget was $1.2 million, Michael White and I could personally guarantee it. If the film didn't get completed or didn't turn out well, we would have been the ones to lose.

John Goldstone We somehow managed to convince Fox that we could make the movie for $1.2 million, which I think was about £750,000 back then. But it was tough, as there were all sorts of pitfalls. Just making a musical with dance numbers is never easy, because it involves rehearsals and a lot of people. And that means money. We had to do things on the cheap.

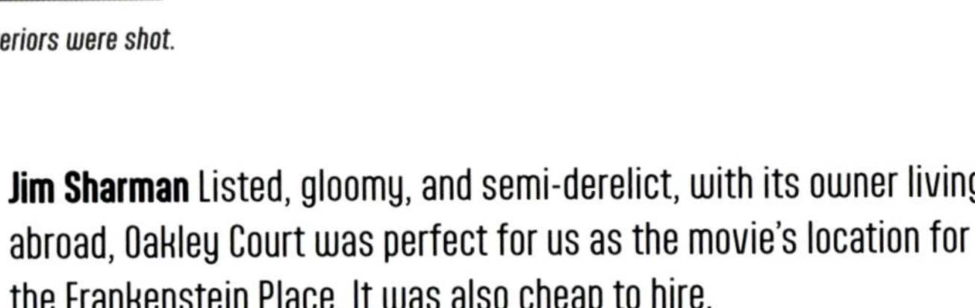

Jim Sharman Listed, gloomy, and semi-derelict, with its owner living abroad, Oakley Court was perfect for us as the movie's location for the Frankenstein Place. It was also cheap to hire.

John Goldstone For the film's location, we found this house in Bray, Berkshire, called Oakley Court. It was a privately owned mansion that had been, for years prior, [used] for Hammer horror films, the British equivalent of Roger Corman. Oakley Court was next door to Bray Studios, which had half a dozen soundstages—big enough for us to build adapted interiors of Oakley Court.

Patricia Quinn One day on set at Bray Studios, Brian Thomson looked out the window at this building, a house, and asked, "What's that place?" They told him it was used in the Hammer horror films. He said, "I'm having that," and that opened up the whole shoot. We took over that amazing building, which was in poor condition. The landowners wanted the house to fall down, but we worked in it despite the rain coming in through the roof.

Susan Sarandon The house we filmed in had been used for horror films before. There was hardly any roof, which was another reason we were freezing. It was leaking everywhere and so cold.

Before filming began in October 1974, Jim and Richard welcomed a few new members into the Rocky *family, including Peter Hinwood as Rocky, Susan Sarandon as Janet, and Barry Bostwick as Brad . . . as well as a bunch of Transylvanians, of course.*

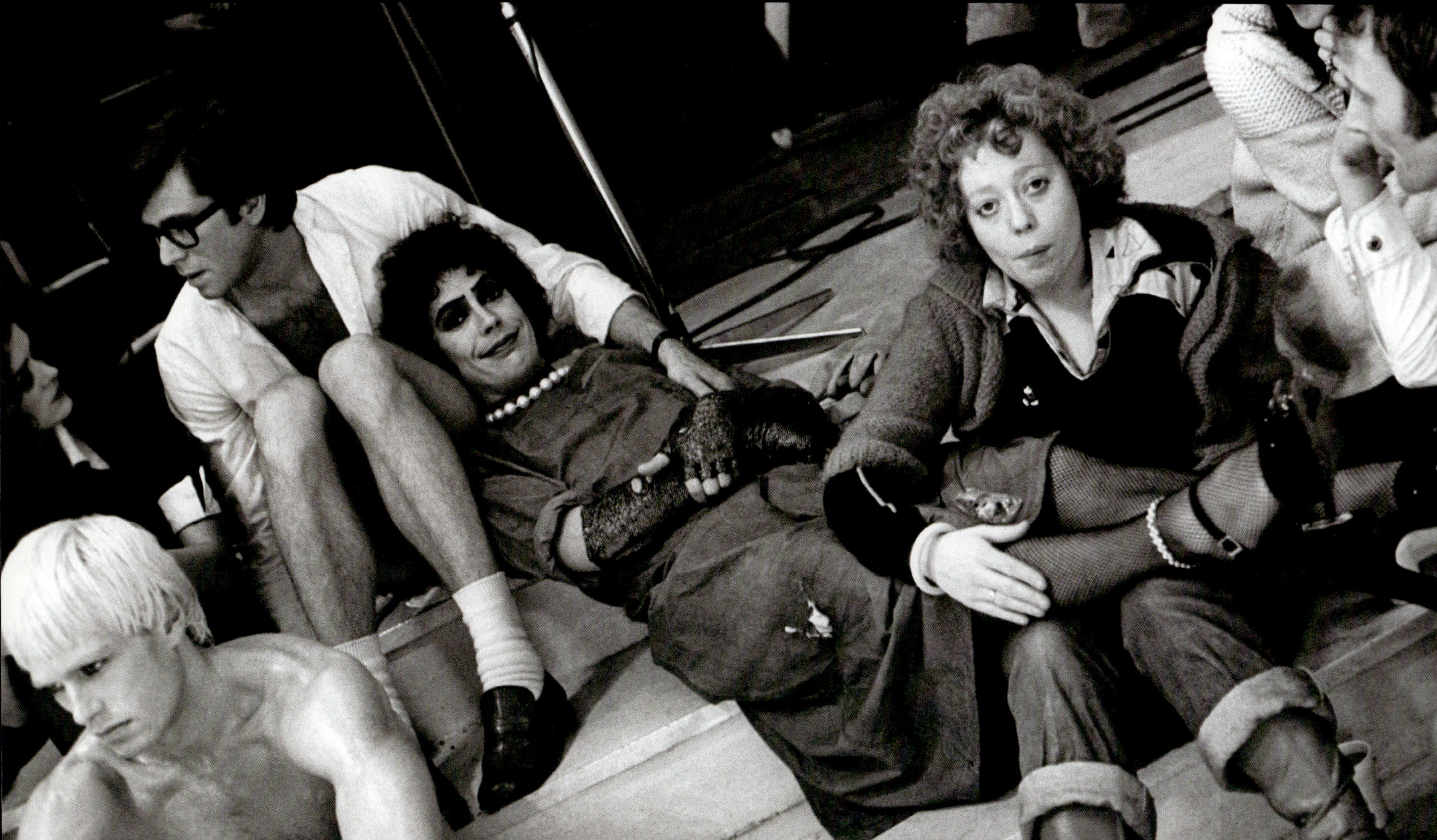

Above: Costume designer Sue Blane (right) takes a break on set with Tim, Barry, Peter, and Patricia.
Following pages: Brad and Janet (Barry Bostwick, Susan Sarandon) meet their host for the evening (Tim Curry).

"Bray Studios was like a soundstage with huts for the wardrobe people, and that was it. There are photos of us all asleep on chairs, some of us lying on the floor. The set had nowhere for us to sit or lie down. It was very basic."

—Patricia Quinn

Good girl gone bad: Janet (Susan Sarandon) goes from being touched up by the makeup artist to touch-a touch-a touched by Rocky (Peter Hinwood).

What Transylvanian conventioneer doesn't know "The Time Warp"?

Barry Bostwick *Rocky* wasn't shocking to me at all. I was a New York actor, and I had done enough off-Broadway to see the underbelly of society. I didn't hesitate at all to doing this movie. It was in my wheelhouse.

Susan Sarandon I've always made career decisions based on how much fun something seemed or whether it was something I hadn't done before. And *The Rocky Horror Picture Show* checked all the boxes.

Barry Bostwick I had done a number of stage roles where you put a layer of comment on top of the reality of it. But that's not what was funny about *Rocky*. What was funny about *Rocky* was that the situation was funny and we had to just play it damn straight.

Susan Sarandon Janet was just a combination of all the ingenues I had been playing up until that time. I started acting when I was twenty, which was about five years earlier than most leading ladies. So I had to make that transition from ingenue to leading lady. But at that point, Janet was still very much in the ingenue category.

Nell Campbell In the movie, the Transylvanians were cast by Jim. He wanted every type of person present to represent the audience so everyone in the audience could identify with them. Another great way of the film being so inclusive.

Jim Sharman I cast a diverse group of people as the Transylvanians, which might resonate even more today. It was meant to be an annual global convention, and I didn't want them to look like a traditional Broadway chorus translated to film. They don't dance in perfect synchronicity—they dance like people at a party. Many things that people assume were errors were actually deliberate choices to subvert the form. I sped up the voices of the Transylvanians because I wanted them to sound like Munchkins. I wanted to create a kind of dark fairy tale, and *The Wizard of Oz* was an influence.

Susan Sarandon I'm sure the previous Janets had the power in their voices to sell the songs. But when people say my voice sounds vulnerable in the movie, it's because I was having a nervous breakdown! I know I'm not a singer.

SYLVANIAN CONVENTION

Above: Eddie (Meat Loaf) gets ready for his entrance.
Following pages: Jim Sharman and Tim Curry chat between takes of the "Sweet Transvestite" sequence.

Opposite: Janet (Susan Sarandon) knows what she wants, and gets it from Rocky (Peter Hinwood).
Above: Jim directing Peter and Tim in Frank's death scene.

Jack Black Meat Loaf as Eddie made a huge impact on me. When I first saw the movie, I felt a psychic connection with him. It was like I was looking at an older version of myself. That stuck with me throughout my youth. When Kyle [Gass] and I were talking about doing a Tenacious D movie, I immediately said, "We've got to get Meat Loaf as my dad." And he did it. During filming, he told me, "This is the first time I've sung in a movie since *Rocky Horror*." It was a weird full-circle moment, as I was a nine-year-old kid watching him as Eddie for the first time.

Nell Campbell Peter Hinwood [Rocky] was the only man with muscles in the whole of the United Kingdom in 1974. He had zero confidence when it came to the Rocky role and was completely insecure about it. Yet he completely nailed the performance.

Peter Hinwood I first heard about the movie when I was asked to audition. I was at a modeling agency, and they called me up and said they wanted me to audition. I was surprised at first, but everyone told me to go ahead, so I did. The audition took place on the corner of Old Church Street and the King's [Road] in the Classic Cinema. That's where I first met Jim Sharman. He wanted me to mime to Bryan Ferry's "The 'In' Crowd"—that's all I had to do! Then they gave me the job. I was terrified, but I took on the challenge.

I was chosen because I had a six-pack. I never considered myself as great as Arnold Schwarzenegger. I went to the gym and lifted weights, but I wasn't anything special.

Trixie Mattel Peter Hinwood—he's so beautiful. I know he's not really an actor, but he's so good in this film, for a nonspeaking role. He's just gorgeous. He speaks to me, mainly because he runs around in his underwear. That part where Frank-N-Furter touches his belly button? Honestly, that's the only moment in the film where I'm like, "Okay, that's hot."

"Ironically, considering *Rocky* was a creation of Frank's, Peter Hinwood—who played Rocky—was the shyest, quietest person. I think filming the 'Touch Me' scene was traumatizing for him."

—Susan Sarandon

DEEP FREEZE

Previous pages: Frank (Tim Curry) marvels at his creation, Rocky (Peter Hinwood).
Opposite: Shooting the opening wedding scene.
Following pages: Frank (Tim Curry) is going home.

"The live show has an energy that the movie doesn't have—it wasn't intentional, but the film is very slow. The movie is a very surreal, almost dreamlike journey; the live show is far more rock and roll."

—Richard O'Brien

Richard O'Brien For the role of Rocky, what we needed was someone that the camera could go around 360 degrees and not have to fudge anywhere. Peter looked good from all angles.

Susan Sarandon Ironically, considering Rocky was a creation of Frank's, Peter Hinwood—who played Rocky—was the shyest, quietest person. I think filming the "Touch Me" scene was traumatizing for him.

Filming of The Rocky Horror Picture Show *began on October 23, 1974, at Oakley Court and Bray Studios near Windsor and, by all accounts, was a triumph of will, to quote Magenta—and a mental mind fuck, as Frank would say.*

Jim Sharman We shot the film chronologically. The early scenes are a little static and slow, but it picks up pace once Brad and Janet get to the castle.

John Goldstone The shoot was a complete nightmare and all kinds of dangerous. But we were all very young and working by the seat of our pants. Every day was just trying to make sure that we were getting through it and delivering good shots.

Patricia Quinn The movie was a six-week shoot—a musical in six weeks. Unheard of. We were worked to exhaustion. It was great, but hard work.

Susan Sarandon I remember the whole experience—except for the pneumonia—being fun. Everything was shot quickly because we had such a tight budget. And I just remember having a good time.

Jeffrey Weinstock Oakley Court was in a state of disrepair—cold, leaky, and lacking any real heating. To help with the conditions, they had a warming room with industrial heaters—until a fire broke out, and that was the end of that.

John Goldstone: The shoot was in autumn in London, and it was cold. We had these rain sequences and a lot of water in the studio. Even the indoor water scenes were very cold. But the actors and crew were all troupers. They were prepared to suffer for their art.

Susan Sarandon I know it was a very tough shoot for Tim. We were working long and uncomfortable hours, and he had so much makeup to go through each time. I just thought it was remarkable that he never seemed to tire, even though it was rough. We didn't have a lot of time to relax.

Barry Bostwick The shoot was quick. I was wet and miserable most of the time, and so was Susan. The most difficult thing for me to deal with during the shoot was dancing on a wet floor in high heels! It had nothing to do with my sexuality or the technical side of actually making the movie. And before each scene, they had to spray me down with cold water, and I was in my underwear the whole time.

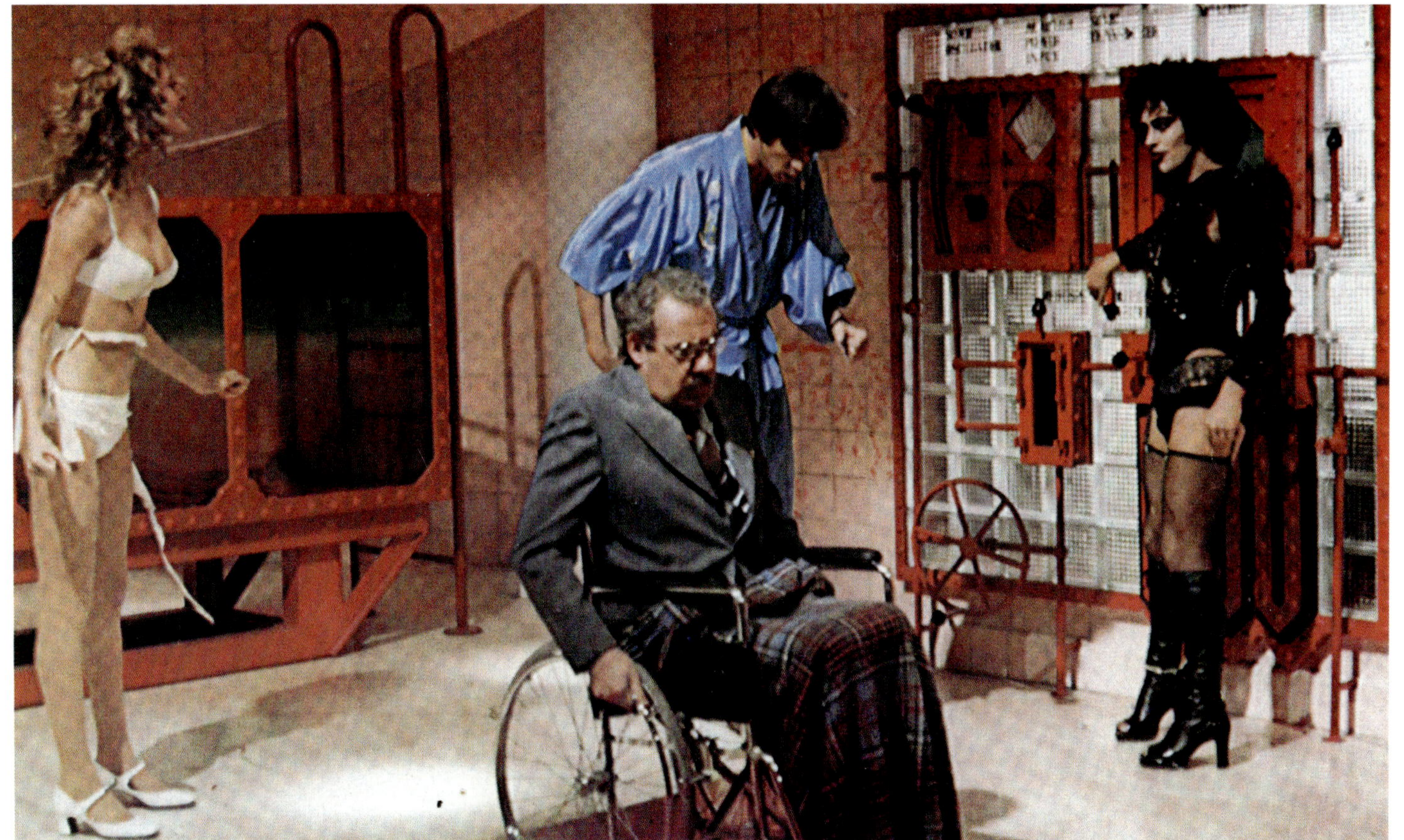

Opposite: Frank's (Tim Curry's) Judy Garland at Carnegie Hall moment .
Above: Dr. Scott (Jonathan Adams), Brad (Barry Bostwick), and Janet (Susan Sarandon) are seduced by Frank's transducer.

Jim Sharman I was happy with everyone in the cast, but I was thrilled with Susan Sarandon. But it was only once we started filming that I realized what a career she was going to have. When I saw her through the camera, I thought, "Those eyes could wipe everyone else off the screen"—and sometimes, they did.

John Goldstone Jim was a very good director. He was well prepared. He would demand and push as far as he possibly could. He would want to do as many takes as possible and keep on shooting as long as we could. Sometimes the cast got a bit fed up with that, but they all got what it was that we were working on.

"The final moments of the film—Frank's final plea—was influenced by conversations between Tim Curry and me, as well as Peter Suschitzky's cinematography. It had a Judy Garland at Carnegie Hall quality to it—that was the territory we were in."

—Jim Sharman

Jack Black At the end, of course, you feel for Frank-N-Furter. You love him because you've gone on this journey with him. Sure, he killed a couple of characters along the way, but he's also an incredible showman.

Barry Bostwick My performance of Brad was based on me echoing my cousin's husband, who was a straight accountant, a throwback to the 1950s. I never told him while he was alive that I was actually copying him. He probably wouldn't have liked that so much.

Brian Thomson Jim came over to me one day and said, "Where's the secret entrance into the lab? You know, the one Dr. Scott comes through." I had forgotten to put it in! Jim looked at me and said, "How are we going to get Dr. Scott into the lab, then?" I was getting a little tired at this point, so I told him, "Just push him through the wall." That's why Jonathan Adams comes flying through the cardboard like that.

Barry Bostwick When I recorded "Once in a While," I thought, "Wow, what a sweet song." And then we recorded it and we shot it, and then I saw the movie and . . . the song wasn't in the movie! It's such a sweet song, but it slowed the movie down immensely. Brad's now talking about his relationship with Janet and what just happened and . . . who gives a shit?

"For the movie, I thought it was very important to turn Frank into an art connoisseur. He and I have similar taste, although Frank goes a little haywire at times. That's why I threw in the Greek sculpture with a Michelangelo and a few Magrittes. It's tasteful, but at the same time it's just a little wrong, a little too eclectic. Did you notice the top hat on one of the griffins in the ballroom? That's a Magritte image. Wonderfully surreal."

—Brian Thomson

Above: Frank's masterpiece, Rocky (Peter Hinwood), marvels at Michelangelo's masterpiece. Opposite: No one wore gloves better.

Jim Sharman My surrealist tendencies definitely came through more in the film. Some ideas were even invented on the spot—like the dinner scene where they eat Eddie. That idea came up the day before shooting. I terrorized everyone so much that day that we got real fear in the scene.

Jeffrey Weinstock Jim Sharman loved playing pranks on set, so none of the other actors knew the body was under the table—except for Tim Curry. So when he pulled the cloth away, their gasps of shock and horror were completely real.

Jim Sharman That was also the day Fox executives visited the set—they took one look and fled in horror.

Jeffrey Weinstock Studio executive Alan Ladd Jr. visited the set once, stayed for about twenty minutes, and then left looking completely bewildered.

Barry Bostwick My favorite moment from the movie is when Tim, right before he reveals his Rocky, pulls on the rubber glove and it snaps. To me, that's the funniest thing in the whole movie. It's just a brilliant moment in the film.

Richard O'Brien The movie was also supposed to be shot in black and white until we throw open the doors in the castle for "The Time Warp"—about twenty minutes in. It was supposed to go to color there, like *Wizard of Oz*. That didn't happen. I believe you can get a DVD now where that's been done. It doesn't make any difference, truthfully.

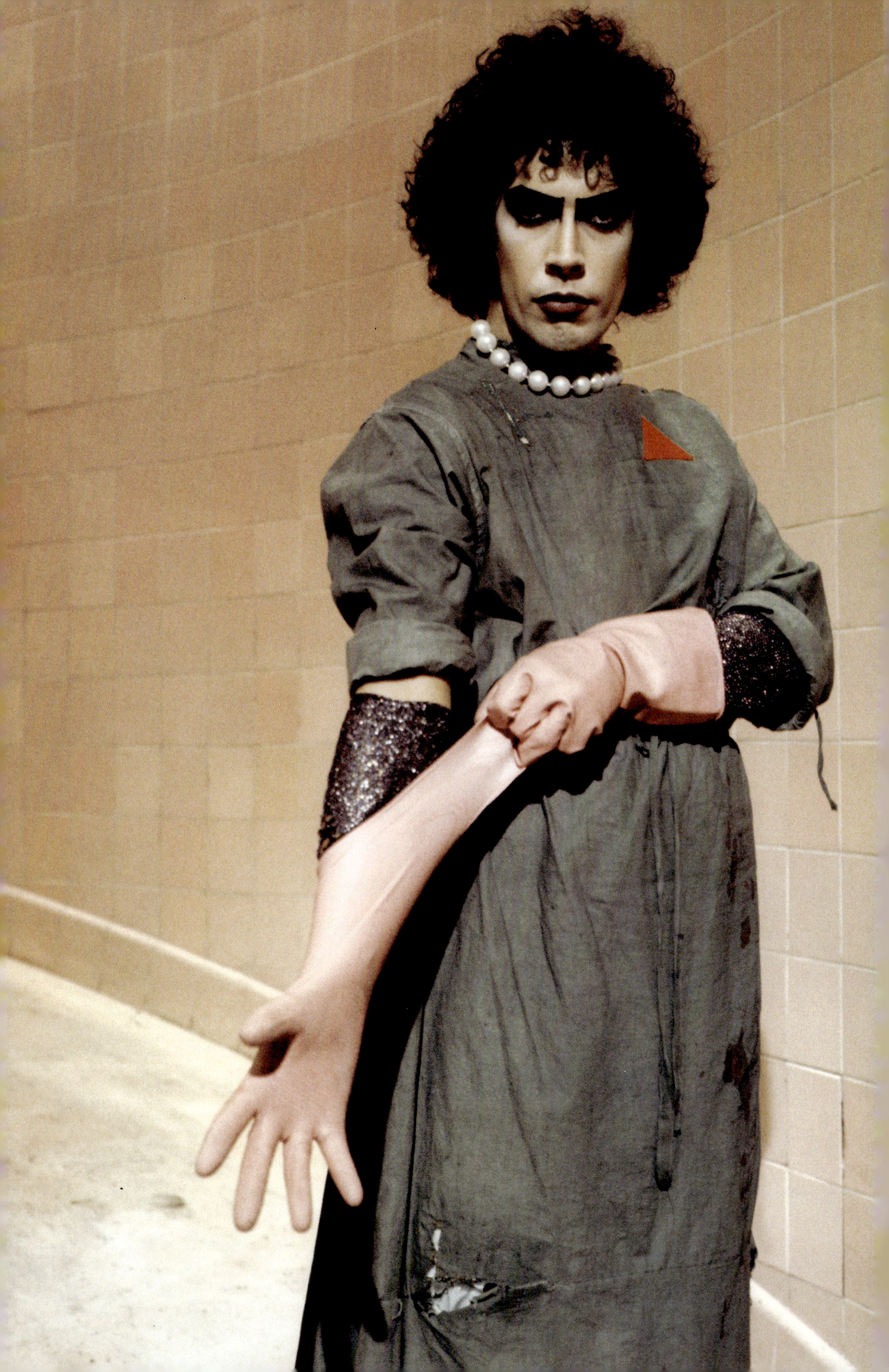

Columbia (Nell Campbell) shows off her tapping skills in "The Time Warp."

"Everyone looked amazing in a corset and fishnets. The men and the women."

—Nell Campbell

The wild and untamed things do a kick line during the floor show.

Picture

Above: Nell Campbell as Columbia, the world's greatest groupie. Opposite: Janet and Brad (Susan Sarandon, Barry Bostwick) in the lab, waiting to see what's on the slab.

Brian Thomson The idea to shoot the first twenty minutes of the movie in black and white was dropped because there was a problem matching in the black and white with the color print. You'll notice that the beginning of the film looks totally washed out. It was done specifically in white, blacks, and grays to contrast with the later ballroom scene, which was suddenly supposed to explode with color.

Nell Campbell Those plaster casts—they're our bodies. We had to stand naked in a pose, be covered in plaster, and wait for it to harden in a freezing-cold room. I think all those plaster casts are in someone's bedroom somewhere in England.

Richard Hartley For the film, we hired the French makeup artist Pierre La Roche. But he took so long that all the actors went back to doing their own makeup.

Susan Sarandon I remember Britt Ekland, Lou Adler's girlfriend. She was on set and said to me, "With those legs, you should always wear heels." I was just like, "Okay, I'll wear heels from now on."

Richard O'Brien The biggest change from stage to screen was switching "The Time Warp" to come before "Sweet Transvestite." The great thing about this change is that the party music plays as Brad and Janet enter the house and start getting involved with these characters, delaying Frank's entrance by a few minutes. That delay builds anticipation—everyone knows he's about to appear, and stretching it out just a bit longer adds to the tension.

Barry Bostwick It was funny: When we were making it, I thought we were making a contemporary *Sound of Music*.

Jim Sharman If I had to choose a favorite nonmusical moment in the film, it would be the "If only, if only, if only" sequence with Janet against the red wall—a little Jean-Luc Godard moment.

Opposite: Tim Curry taking a break during the pool scene.
Above: Shooting "Sweet Transvestite."

Richard O'Brien My favorite shot in the movie is when the smoke billows above the swimming pool. The camera is above, looking straight down, and as the smoke disappears, there's Frank on top of the pool in that *Titanic* pose, with the God and Adam motif at the base. It's a million-dollar shot, even though the whole film was made for just a little over a million and a quarter dollars. But that shot alone was worth a million.

Patricia Quinn On the last day of shooting, Jim Sharman called me over and asked, "Have you ever seen Man Ray's lips painting?" I knew of it. "I have this idea," he said. "I was wondering if your mouth could sing 'Science Fiction/Double Feature.' " "My mouth and Richard's voice?" I asked. I'd been furious about not singing "Science Fiction," and this was his way of making it up to me. "Your lips will sing the song," he said. I went home and forgot about it. A few months later, I'm called to go to Elstree Studios to lip-sync the song. There were no special effects, so they blacked out my face, drew muscle lines to guide the shot, and covered the camera with cloth to focus only on my mouth. They clamped my head in place. A big arc lamp lit my lips, and that's how the *Rocky Horror* lips special effect was created for the opening sequence.

Jim Sharman Wally Veevers, who worked on *2001: A Space Odyssey*, was handling the special effects for the movie. He was a wonderful presence in the studio but was horrified by how low-budget our effects were. Still, I'll never forget the day we shot "Sweet Transvestite." Wally, who rarely smiled, was absolutely beaming. I asked him why, and he said, "I haven't seen anything like this on a soundstage since the days of Josef von Sternberg and Marlene Dietrich." That was one of the greatest compliments I ever received.

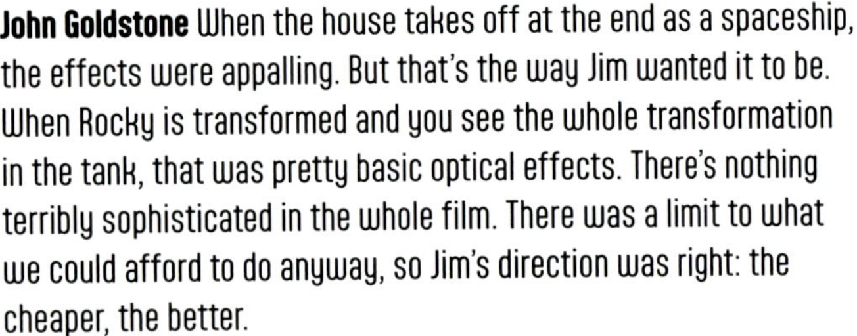

Eddie (Meat Loaf) feels the wrath of Frank's (Tim Curry's) wrath—and glee.

John Goldstone When the house takes off at the end as a spaceship, the effects were appalling. But that's the way Jim wanted it to be. When Rocky is transformed and you see the whole transformation in the tank, that was pretty basic optical effects. There's nothing terribly sophisticated in the whole film. There was a limit to what we could afford to do anyway, so Jim's direction was right: the cheaper, the better.

Jim Sharman Some people think elements of the movie feel like a B-movie because of bad filmmaking—but that was deliberate. For instance, the special effects team was shocked when I told them their work was too good. I said, "No, the effects have to be really bad." That said, some parts do look like a B-movie simply because we were working on a B-picture budget and schedule. Some things were deliberately B-movie, while others genuinely resulted from the limitations. Although I can't tell you which were which. Life is full of contradictions and so is *The Rocky Horror Picture Show*.

I knew there would be little interference from the studio, Fox. The studio saw it as such a minor investment that they just let us do our thing. Whether it was that or Lou Adler keeping them at bay, there was *zero* studio interference. For better or worse, we made the film exactly as we intended. And, as it turns out—for better.

Despite the film's flawless performances—every cast member delivers a star turn—it was Tim Curry's enthralling execution of the egomaniac Frank that once again became the toast of popular conversation, with the actor lauded then, and now, not just for guaranteeing **Rocky Horror's** ***immortality, but also for igniting the flame of gender on film for generations to follow.***

Jeffrey Weinstock The moment Frank-N-Furter throws off his cloak and reveals himself as a transvestite in such a direct, confrontational way—that's a pivotal moment in film history. It challenged all gender norms.

Above and following pages: Scientist, lover, host, master, and sweet transvestite: a gallery of Dr. Frank-N-Furter (Tim Curry).

BOSS

Jim Sharman I wanted to hold off Frank's entrance until about fifteen minutes in—because that's when it would happen in a late-night movie tradition.

Trixie Mattel When you watch Tim Curry do Frank-N-Furter, it's a bipartisan issue. I don't care how homophobic or conservative you are—there's something about him. The moment he walks onscreen, it's not about gender.

Jack Black Tim Curry's performance as Frank-N-Furter is so iconic. If that was the only film Tim ever did, he would still be one of the greats of cinema. His performance is dripping with charisma. You can't take your eyes off him, hanging on every word. He introduced the world to a new kind of sexuality, giving people permission to be whatever they want to be.

Susan Sarandon Watching Tim work was like a master class. I've seen many people play Frank-N-Furter, but none of them have his charisma.

Barry Bostwick Every song that Tim Curry sang I wanted to sing.

John Goldstone Frank-N-Furter's entrance—which had been so incredible in the stage play, walking down the aisle among the audience—had to be totally reconceived. But it didn't matter, because we attacked it with the same spirit as the show. And pulled it off.

Patricia Quinn Tim delivered an extraordinary, masterful performance. But when you're acting alongside him, you're not thinking, "Oh, isn't that actor marvelous?" You're just acting with them. You're not being objective about it. I wasn't standing there amazed by him.

John Goldstone Tim's first appearance in the movie is mind-blowing—definitely my favorite moment in the film. He knew what he was doing; he just brought something to that character that had an authority and believability. He was very much in charge.

Sean Waters I was completely captivated by Tim's entrance as Frank. What is he? Who is he? What is he going to do next? What is he going to say next? Who is he going to fuck? Who is he going to kill? You can't take your eyes off him. Tim Curry was more than just the right actor for the right part. He was born to be Frank.

Jeffrey Weinstock The moment Frank throws off his cloak in the elevator is when the audience truly realize they're not in Kansas anymore. It's a brilliant revelation, signaling how the film is going to bend conventional gender norms. Today, with something like *RuPaul's Drag Race*, this kind of gender play isn't as shocking. But I think *Rocky* paved the way for that.

Jim Sharman Editing the film wasn't too difficult because there was very little coverage—we essentially edited in-camera. The only time I went overboard was during Rocky's birth scene. In that moment, I suddenly felt connected to Frankenstein, so I shot a lot more coverage than usual. In fact, I remember sitting in the back of a limousine with Michael White and Lou Adler, asking them to speed up the editing process. Strangely, that scene ended up being the only one with truly elaborate coverage.

THE ROCKY
HORROR
PICTURE SHOW
a different
set of jaws
R RESTRICTED
Under 17 requires accompanying Parent or Adult Guardian
20th CENTURY FOX

The original poster for the movie, with a tagline referencing the blockbuster Jaws, which had just opened a few months before.

The Rocky Horror Picture Show ***completed principal photography on December 21, 1974, and had its world premiere in London on August 14, 1975. The completion of the film heralded the beginning of a new chapter. As the stage show had been a sensational success, expectations for the film's reviews and box office were high. Thankfully, everybody loved it. Right?***

John Goldstone We showed the film to Fox during the mixing stage. If I remember correctly, they didn't understand it at all.

Lou Adler In America, we previewed the film in Santa Barbara, and before that, I had shown it to the marketing and sales department at 20th Century Fox, possibly in a small theater on the lot with maybe one hundred people. The response was deafening silence. Slowly, people began to get up and leave, but nobody said anything to me.

Patricia Quinn The first time I saw the film with the fans was in Leicester Square. I sat with some people from the audience, and they were all saying, "Oh, the show is so much better." I thought, "No, it wasn't." I loved the movie. It was great.

Tim Curry I do remember seeing the film for the first time. There was a screening of it in London. I hated it. I didn't know quite what I expected, but I didn't think we'd pulled it off.

Nell Campbell I cannot bear seeing myself ever on a screen of any kind. I didn't see the movie for twenty-five years!

Belinda Sinclair I thought they did a brilliant job translating it to film. It's rare that a play adapts so well into movies, but they nailed it.

Nell Campbell It was Brian Thomson who, for the first poster of the film, suggested "A different set of jaws." Because, at that time, *Jaws* was the biggest film in the world.

Richard Hartley I don't think any of us felt the film was a success when we first saw it. It was slow. I went to the premiere in London, but I was a bit down about the whole thing.

Barry Bostwick I don't even remember the movie opening. I don't remember it actually having a premiere in the United States.

Jim Sharman I always had faith in the originality of the film and felt it would ultimately find its audience, but the early signs weren't good. I don't think we knew quite what to expect when the movie first opened.

"When I first saw the film, I said, 'Yeah, it looks terrific, it sounds terrific, but God, look at me, look at Riff Raff.' I agonized over my performance. 'Why did I do that movement? I'm not any good.' You can't concentrate on the film when you are the one who's up there onscreen."

—Richard O'Brien

The Handyman and the Domestic, who have evil schemes of their own: Riff Raff (Richard O'Brien) and Magenta (Patricia Quinn).

CHAPTER 5

SPACED-OUT SENSATION

Great Scott! With the film a flop, *Rocky*'s future began to flounder. Thankfully, its fortunes flourished after a 20th Century Fox executive had a fantastic thought. With it, a brand-new phenomenon was majestically birthed—the midnight movie cult—and so, too, were the audience rituals and shadow cast performances that guaranteed *Rocky* would never walk the same way again.

ACTION PACKED
LOTSA LARFS & SEX
GORGEOUS GALS
THRILLS & CHILLS
TRANSYLVANIAN PARTIES
ROMANCE
Plus 18 Great Songs
TWENTIETH CENTURY FOX PRESENTS
A MICHAEL WHITE–LOU ADLER PRODUCTION
The ROCKY HORROR Picture SHOW AA
A Musical Dream Come True
DOLBY SYSTEM
ORIGINAL MUSICAL PLAY MUSIC AND LYRICS BY RICHARD O'BRIEN
SCREENPLAY BY JIM SHARMAN & RICHARD O'BRIEN
MUSICAL ARRANGEMENTS RICHARD HARTLEY
PRODUCTION SERVICES BY RUBY SERVICE COMPANY
ASSOCIATE PRODUCER JOHN GOLDSTONE
EXECUTIVE PRODUCER LOU ADLER
DIRECTED BY JIM SHARMAN
PRODUCED BY MICHAEL WHITE
'THE ROCKY HORROR PICTURE SHOW' AA
STARRING
TIM CURRY • SUSAN SARANDON • BARRY BOSTWICK
RICHARD O'BRIEN • PATRICIA QUINN • LITTLE NELL
JONATHAN ADAMS • PETER HINWOOD • MEATLOAF • CHARLES GRAY
EASTMAN COLOUR
RELEASED BY FOX-RANK DISTRIBUTORS
ORIGINAL FILM SOUNDTRACK LP ON ODE 78332

Like Eddie, The Rocky Horror Picture Show *was effectively dead on arrival when it was released into the wild in August 1975. The film's initial failure, of course, only kept its immortality on ice until its righteous rebirth a year later. But we'll get to that.*

Richard O'Brien The movie opened . . . and bombed.

Tim Curry I was very depressed. I was miserable. The film was a flop. I took it quite personally. Which is arrogant, but I did. But now, after all these years, I'm completely validated.

Susan Sarandon I wasn't shocked that *Rocky Horror* flopped at first. It just kind of disappeared.

John Goldstone Michael and I were very disappointed when the film wasn't an immediate hit. You put so much into something; you think an audience is going to get it immediately and embrace it. And the film will make zillions. But it did the opposite.

Sue Blane The movie wasn't a success. It wasn't well received in the UK. It pretty much closed a couple of days after its premiere.

Nell Campbell When the film flopped, it was a still a hit show in the West End. I accepted that people for some reason didn't get or appreciate the film, but the show was still a gigantic hit—it just didn't make any sense.

"The fact that it was such an unusual film and that it was devoid of conventional movie stars didn't help. The fashion of the day was for realist films, and this was . . . something else. The mainstream audience only saw the surface, and they turned away; but the late-night audience picked up on what was under that surface—and it spoke to them."

—Jim Sharman

Opposite and above: Two posters, with two very different approaches.

Joel Thurm I was bummed out when the film didn't succeed right away. I thought it should have been a hit, and I couldn't understand why it wasn't.

Susan Sarandon At first, nobody knew what to do with the movie. My agents believed they were right all along. However, they just didn't have the vision to see what it could turn into.

It was great where it all began: The Waverly Theatre in New York City was the first to do midnight showings of Rocky Horror.

Barry Bostwick I didn't even know the movie came out. To me, the movie was just a one-off. It was a movie that was fun to do, but I had no stake in it.

John Goldstone I never really understood quite why the audience didn't pick up on the movie from day one. I assumed we were more liberal in our views than our average audience was.

Nell Campbell In August 1975, the show was still going strong as a hugely successful musical. Sadly, 20th Century Fox gave the film a very limited run in the UK, and an equally extremely limited run in the United States—and it was quickly shelved.

Karen Tongson The movie didn't do very well upon its initial release because it came at the tail end of the movie musical era. People weren't really going to see movie musicals at the time—*Hello, Dolly!* with Barbra Streisand, for example, flopped at the theater just a few years before. People were drawn to other genres of cinema at that time.

Jeffrey Weinstock One major aspect of the cinematography—something that might have contributed to *Rocky Horror's* initial box office failure—was its attempt to mimic the clunkiness of 1950s and '60s B-movies. It wasn't shot like a typical slick Hollywood production. Instead, it leaned into a deliberately campy, low-budget aesthetic.

John Goldstone Back then, you couldn't show films on television for seven years after they were released. So if the movie didn't work in the cinema from day one, you lost all your money.

Patricia Quinn I didn't expect to do anything else with *Rocky* after the movie. I'd finished the work, it was over, and everything went silent. Then the team at Fox shelved it. They didn't know where to put it. They didn't know what to do with it.

Jeffrey Weinstock Critics didn't know what to make of the film. The majority of the reviews were brutal. They called it amateurish, tasteless, tactless. Some said it wasn't funny enough; others said it wasn't sexy enough. It was panned across the board and quickly pulled before the end of October due to poor box office performance.

Tim Curry I did distance myself somewhat from Frank after the movie came out. It was necessary, really, because I wanted to do other things.

Richard Hartley The live show was still doing great business. I didn't think too much of it when the film flopped, but then things changed in a way I could never imagine.

John Goldstone When the film floundered, it was forced to find its own identity. Lou [Adler, the film's executive producer] did enormous things to make that work.

Now a creature of legend in the movie industry, Rocky Horror *is the longest-running theatrical release in the history of cinema. This is all thanks to the creatures of the night, the besotted fans who returned to the movie on multiple occasions for weekend midnight screenings. The first midnight screening occurred on—of course—April Fools' Day, the first of April 1976, at the Waverly Theater in New York's Greenwich Village.*

John Goldstone *Rocky* is the major cult movie of all time. But filmmakers don't make cults. Audiences made cults.

Nell Campbell No one would ever have heard of the film again but for an advertising executive that worked at 20th Century Fox—Tim Deegan. He took it off the shelf, saw it, and thought that would work well as a midnight movie. That man is wholly responsible for how big the film got.

Joel Thurm In a weird twist of fate, while I was working on the show at the Roxy in LA, I rented my guest apartment to Tim Deegan,

WAVERLY
THE ROCKY HORROR PICTURE SHOW
MIDNIGHT SHOW

PARAMOUNT
ROCKY HORROR
BIRTHDAY PARTY 9:00
CHEECH 'N CHONG
PARAMOUNT
CHEECH AND CHONG
MIDNITE
BIRTHDAY 9:00
PARAMOUNT
FIRE ZONE

In April 1977, the Paramount in Austin, Texas, hosted the first Rocky Horror Birthday Party and Costume Ball. The sold-out event included a special appearance by Tim Curry.

vice president of advertising at 20th Century Fox. It was him who came up with the idea for the midnight screenings.

Lou Adler The only executive from Fox who attended the preview in Santa Barbara was a young guy, Tim Deegan. By halfway through the film, we had lost half the audience. By the end, Tim and I were despondent, sitting on the curb outside the theater trying to figure out what to do next. That's when college kids started coming up to us and saying things like, "I love the music" and "I really like this film." Those positive reactions gave us hope that we had a film for a specific audience. We just had to find that audience.

Tim Deegan After a poor box office showing in Los Angeles and a failed test market for a college audience in Columbus, Ohio, the studio shelved the movie. Everyone at Fox was scared stiff of being associated with a gay movie, which is how they perceived it. "Sweet Transvestite" was a song that gave them shivers. The movie was doomed from the start, but I was totally convinced there was a midnight audience.

Lou Adler At the time, Fox wouldn't dare play midnight screenings, but Tim Deegan had an idea. He had a friend in New York who was an exhibitor, and they suggested, "Why don't we try a midnight screening? It can't hurt." That was a big turning point for *Rocky Horror*. It gave the film life.

Jeffrey Weinstock Tim Deegan was really the only one paying attention to what was happening—especially in Los Angeles, where people were coming back to see the film multiple times. Midnight screenings were already becoming popular in the 1970s as a way to showcase offbeat, cult, and campy films. It was Deegan who reached out to the Waverly Theater in Manhattan about screening *Rocky Horror* as a midnight movie.

Tim Deegan The movie was so unique that once audiences "discovered" it, word of mouth would carry it. My marketing plan was two-pronged: no advertising, and you can only see it at midnight. No studio had ever played a movie at midnight. It was an instant success.

"Someone in London asked me, 'Have you heard what's happening to your movie in the States?' I thought, 'It's gone down the tubes, right?' But they said, 'No, quite the opposite.' Then they told me about the late-night screenings and how it was taking off. It was Tim Deegan, the chap at Fox, who had the bright idea to try the midnight circuits—and he hit it right on the head."

—Richard O'Brien

John Goldstone At first, I didn't understand what the midnight screenings were. It sounded like a bit of a cop-out. Why not just show the film inside normal hours? But it was smart: The audience found it, embraced it, and made it into something completely different.

Sal Piro On April Fools' Day, 1976, Tim Deegan persuaded Bill Quigley of the Walter Reade Organization to replace the midnight show at the Waverly Theater with *Rocky*. The Waverly had already been a mecca for midnight movies and had had two very successful runs of *El Topo* and *Night of the Living Dead*. The manager of the Waverly, Denise Borden, was fascinated with the film and began her own personal hype campaign, with photos in the box office window and a theater telephone recording that stated, "This is a film not to be missed."

Sal Piro.

"When the midnight screenings finally took off, there were theaters all across America, especially in the Midwest, that would have shut down if it weren't for *Rocky Horror* playing at midnight on Fridays and Saturdays. *Rocky* helped save the very theaters that had originally inspired it."

—Jim Sharman

Jeffrey Weinstock Sal Piro, a *Rocky Horror* superfan and president of the fan club, played a key role in this as well. At some point, the idea emerged: Why don't we put together a cast to act along with the film? It didn't happen all at once—it seems like the shadow cast concept developed in bits and pieces over time.

Sean Waters Sal Piro was a very big part of the midnight screenings' success. We called him Big Papa.

Lou Adler Sal Piro loved *Rocky Horror*. The myth is that he was on his way to becoming a priest and was attending seminary when a friend took him to see *Rocky Horror*. After seeing it, he realized what he truly wanted to do and became the fan club leader, remaining a part of it for fifty years, until he passed away [in January 2023]. He stayed involved with *Rocky Horror* until the very end, continuing to participate just as he did in the early days. He organized the fan club and exposed the film to new audiences. He was incredibly special to the *Rocky Horror* community.

Jeffrey Weinstock When it first premiered as a midnight movie at the Waverly, the audience was small—but what they quickly noticed was that people kept coming back the next week, and they were bringing friends with them. The audience wasn't just showing up—it was growing.

Lou Adler An exhibitor in Austin, Texas, decided to take a chance based on the success of the midnight screening in New York. Tim Deegan and I split up the calls to both cities. He'd check in with New York, and I'd check in with Austin. After about the third call to Austin, I asked how it was going. The manager said, "About fifty people." I said, "Fifty people?" He said, "Yeah, but what's interesting, it's the same fifty people every week." That's when I knew something special was starting.

Meat Loaf I went to a sold-out midnight screening one time in 1978 in New York with a bunch of friends. I told the manager that I'm in the movie, but he didn't believe me! I finally convinced them. "You better be, Meat Loaf! 'Cause we're sitting you at the front!" They sat me next to these two people who said they had seen the film 220 times in a row, and who were snorting cocaine throughout the movie, getting really into it. The fans, the screenings, everything, it was total insanity.

Tim Curry When I first heard about the midnight screenings in the 1980s, I went to the Waverly. I was living in New York at the time. One weekend, I decided to go with some friends. I called the cinema and told the manager, "Hello, my name is Tim Curry, and I've heard about your midnight screenings and would love to see one." The voice on the phone said, "You're the third Tim Curry that's called today." "Well, this is the real one," I replied. When I arrived, the usher reluctantly showed us to our seats. The audience recognized me and some people came up, touched me, and giggled—it was a strange feeling. Then the manager appeared, saying, "You're an impostor and need to leave." I showed her my passport and said, "I'm not an impostor." She said, "Okay, fine. Sit down." So we stayed and watched the whole movie, intrigued by the audience's participation—holding up toast, umbrellas, and doing all the things they do.

Lillias Piro From the first time I saw *Rocky Horror* in March of '77, I made sure that I was getting into the Village as much as possible to see the film. I was at the Waverly a lot. I was there the night Tim Curry was there. Tim Curry showed up incognito. Somebody knew it was him. We all very quickly heard Tim Curry was in the audience, and everybody was out of their minds. I think they threw him out because he was creating such a stir!

Jeffrey Weinstock There was about a nine-month gap between the film's withdrawal and its rebirth as a cult hit. By the end of 1978, there were fifty prints in circulation, and from there, it just kept growing.

Richard Hartley I didn't hear about the midnight screenings until 1979. Richard, Patricia, and I were invited to this convention in New York. I didn't really hear about them at the time; I was busy with other things. But I went. Then they ran the film, and I sat next to Richard, and we just watched. I'd never seen anything like it in my life! It was like the days of Shakespeare when audiences would eat, drink, and shout out. It was a movie, and the audience was getting up, walking around, shouting incredibly funny lines. I'd never seen anything like it—truly unique. I don't think there's another film that has that kind of audience interaction.

"Movie theaters could rely on a packed house on Fridays and Saturdays, which enabled them to survive. So *Rocky* ends up saving not only the lives of individuals—it ends up saving the cinemas that it was celebrating. It's the gift that keeps on giving!"

—Nell Campbell

Susan Sarandon When the movie was resurrected, I was amazed. We couldn't have planned for that. It was unexpected, but also incredible. Sometimes it takes years for things to show you why they were a good thing. I'm just happy that it came back.

Joel Thurm By the time I saw the audience participation at midnight screenings in the '80s, it wasn't organic anymore. It had already become a thing. I wish I'd seen it from the start. That's when I realized it was a cultural phenomenon.

Jim Sharman *Rocky Horror* took a while to become a cult film. It didn't happen overnight. The stage show hadn't done well on Broadway, but there was an audience interested in it. That audience became the midnight screening crowd.

Opposite: Audience partici . . . pation: throwing rice during the wedding scene, and Brad and Janet's walk through the rain.
Above: Dori Hartley as Frank-N-Furter with other shadow cast members.

In April 1977, at the Waverly Theater, New York, devoted audience members, such as lifelong superfans Sal Piro and Dori Hartley, began interacting within the movie, throwing items at certain points within the film, bringing bags full of props—such as cards, newspapers, and umbrellas—and yelling lines of "counter-dialogue" at characters on the screen. Rocky had entered a new, exciting era of audience participation, and it's one that endures to this day.

Jeffrey Weinstock A kindergarten teacher from Staten Island named Louis Farese started the audience callouts at the Waverly in April 1977, according to the legend.

Sal Piro At the Waverly, audiences began to respond naturally to the film by booing the villain and cheering the heroes. This spawned a whole group of regulars who weekly reserved the same seats in the first row of the balcony. These pioneers of audience participation from the balcony included two young ladies named Amy and Theresa, Bill O'Brien—the first person to dress as Dr. Frank-N-Furter—Lori Davis, and Louis Farese.

On May 1, 1976, Louis felt compelled to speak to the screen. He is credited as the first person to yell lines at the movie. His earliest lines were: "Buy an umbrella, you cheap bitch!" to Janet walking in the rain, and "How strange was it?" to the Criminologist's initial speech. Louis called this "counterpoint dialogue." Then, in late September, as they sought a preview of Halloween, a few people came dressed as characters from the movie. Later, on Halloween, there was a costume party with many people dressing as the characters.

Jim Sharman The film's a bit long, and it's so slow. It wilts after an hour, then picks up again. That might explain why audience participation started to play a big part at screenings—they probably got bored, so they started answering back.

Sal Piro The first time I heard Louis Farese's voice speaking back to the screen, it was funny and I was delighted. Suddenly I was ten years old again. The whole theater rocked with laughter. As the film continued, I wanted to shout out something clever too, but I didn't have the nerve. By my third viewing, I was ready to try my hand at an original line. When Frank asked, "Whatever happened to Fay Wray?," I answered, "She went apeshit!"—exactly what the audience did when they heard me. This was the first of dozens of lines that I created. Some of them were forgotten, but plenty of them are still shouted out in theaters across the country today.

Barry Bostwick The movie has so many pauses, it allowed the audience to yell at us.

Richard O'Brien The first time I saw the crowd participate so intensely was at a convention in Long Island. There were at least a thousand people there. After a Q&A, they showed the movie on a big

Left and below: Shadow cast players from the New York City showings at the Waverly and the 8th Street Playhouse.
Following pages: Transylvanians as far as the eye can see: a typical New York City audience.

stage, and a Frank-N-Furter impersonator, Dori Hartley, dressed exactly like him, performed during the "I'm Going Home" moment. The real-life Dori, in a spotlight, mimicked Tim's movements perfectly. Her silhouette on the screen matched Frank-N-Furter's exactly. The audience sang along, and I realized: This was theater at its finest. It was a spontaneous blend of live theater, audience, and cinema that couldn't have been rehearsed. It was remarkable.

Richard Hartley The film is slow. There are so many long pauses. Some of it looks quite deliberate—you'd think the editor would have cut them shorter. Fans started to fill those gaps. They were sitting there thinking, "Oh my God, when is this going to end." And then, little by little, it caught on. Now I think the audience is as important as the stage show itself.

Susan Sarandon Now, screenings are a little more chaotic, with everyone just screaming things all over. But in the early days, especially in New York, there was a very tight structure to the audience responses. I was floored by the audience more than anything.

Jack Black I was nine when I first saw *The Rocky Horror Picture Show*, around 1978–'79. I was definitely the youngest person in the audience, but it was a trip! People were acting crazy when the movie began with the wedding scene, and throwing rice. I remember thinking, "Everyone has already seen this movie. They're doing stuff because they know the next line!" I was amazed by the audience just as much as by the movie itself. No one was sitting down. It felt like a rock concert.

Tim Curry The audience participation didn't make me like the movie any more, although it was nice to see the film's impact on people, and quite encouraging in a way.

Trixie Mattel The callbacks are the best! There's one where Brad says, "I've done a lot," and everyone shouts, "Cheap gay sex!"

"I remember when David Bowie came to a midnight screening at the height of the film's popularity at the Waverly, and he brought this huge entourage and his wife, Angie, with him. When Riff Raff was about to kill me, Angie shouted, 'No! No! Don't do it!' So I guess she was one of the first people to do that."

—Nell Campbell

Barry Bostwick To me, there's two groups of fans. There are the shadow cast fans, who are the ones who are really affected by it. And then there are the people who go out into the audience in jokes, throw shit at the screen, and are out there drunk, stoned, and having a good time.

Nell Campbell I first heard about the audience participation when I was in Australia. My agent called and said, "An American entrepreneur wants to fly you to New York for a first anniversary midnight screening celebration of *The Rocky Horror Picture Show*." I'll say yes to almost anything in life, especially if it comes with an air ticket. So off I went to New York, and the entrepreneur turned out to be a sixteen-year-old boy named John Mandracchia. Meat Loaf, Brian Thomson, Patricia, Jonathan Adams [who played Dr. Everett Scott], Sue Blane, and the two Richards were there too. It was fantastic. The event was on Long Island at some huge place, and we all rolled up. None of us had ever seen people dressed in our costumes before, so it was huge. We were so excited. Lots of Frank-N-Furters and Riff Raffs. That was the first time I knew the film was going to be okay in the long run.

Above, opposite, and following pages: Shadow casts are still going strong, and getting even more elaborate with their staging.

Patricia Quinn I went to the same New York midnight screening as Nell and Richard [O'Brien] to see what was going on with the audience participation. We couldn't imagine it. Then saw it for ourselves. Fans, in costume, acting it all out, dressing up as me and acting in front of the screen. Crazy. And then it just became normal. That's what people did.

Belinda Sinclair When I saw the movie in New York a couple of years later at a midnight showing, I was blown away. That was also the first time I saw the audience participation—something that never happened in London. Everyone just sat there, shocked. When I saw people showing up in costume, knowing all the lines, throwing rice, and participating, I thought, "Wow, that's amazing."

Susan Sarandon I didn't see it in a theater until it was resurrected—when the midnight screenings had started. I think it was when I took my son to see it at a little cinema on Eighth Street [in New York]. By then, the audience participation was in full swing, and the crowd was so disciplined.

Patricia Quinn I was in London in 1976, having completely forgot about *Rocky Horror*, when someone said, "Have you heard people are dressing up as you?" I thought, "What? What are you talking about?"

Barry Bostwick I'm not quite sure it's justifiable to call my character an asshole! You could call him a bigot, a misogynist. But just because he doesn't have a tire that is fully inflated, to call him an asshole I think was wrong. I want Brad to be called his "Ass Holiness." From now on, I am his Ass Holiness, not just an asshole. I think "asshole" is better than "slut," though, isn't it? I mean, slut. That's really mean-spirited.

Lou Adler Once the midnight screening started in New York, audience participation just steamrolled. They became a fixture, and theaters could continue showing their regular films during the day while running *Rocky Horror* at midnight. It was a win-win—they were making more money with two different types of audiences. For example, in Los Angeles, the Tiffany Theater was running *Rocky Horror* at midnight, sometimes at 2 a.m. or even 4 a.m. So even though we had these odd times, they were still getting their three-show rotation, which everyone was amazed by. We couldn't have sustained an audience or given them the *Rocky Horror* experience with regular daytime screenings. It needed the midnight showings to keep that unique energy alive.

Sue Blane I'll never forget the first time I saw it with fans. It was absolutely bizarre to see them all costumed in front of the real film. It was surreal. On one level, it was quite spectacular. Not only did

they do terribly well, it was really cleverly done. Naively, perhaps, but they put together the costumes as best they could.

Lou Adler What was particularly interesting was how quickly the audience participation began. That simple moment spread to other theaters in different cities. There was a sense of unity in the crowd. As the film gained traction in different cities and more venues picked it up, the audience was consistently the same—people who were excited to join in, to participate. They didn't need us to tell them what to do; they took it upon themselves.

Susan Sarandon The audience participation and callouts are almost like attending church. There's this ritual to it—talking back to the screen, knowing the callouts, the ceremonies. And in that space, you're accepted. And you don't have to go to Burning Man or spend $5,000 going out to the desert for it. You can just be there—be accepted for who you are.

Jack Black With all the audience callouts and interaction with the movie, I knew I was witnessing something special. I was dancing, jumping around, and participating, just like everyone else, having a great time. A lot of the jokes and references went over my head, but it felt like they were breaking all the rules. Norms were being shattered in a naughty, fun way.

Jim Sharman These days, though, the show seems to have become captive to the film. We created a haunted cinema inside a theater, and then theaters became haunted cinemas, and cinemas became theaters as audiences took over and turned the movie into a backdrop for a party. There's a fascinating contradiction there, and a lot of fun in that transition.

Two years after the film was released in the United States, a phenomenon began in New York that had never happened with any other movie before: shadow cast performances. A cast of superfans, dressed as characters from the movie, act out the movie in front of the movie while also interacting with the audience. Put simply: It's a play within a play within a play within a play within, well, you get the picture.

Nell Campbell Today, we now have the audience and the shadow cast perform *Rocky Horror* in front of a screen which is showing *Rocky Horror*. It's an endless loop. The genesis for *Rocky Horror* was Richard going to see all these '50s B-movies, and now you have this complete full circle where it goes from cinema being the inspiration to the stage play that references the movies being an inspiration. And then you have people performing it in front of the screen. It's mind-boggling.

Jeffrey Weinstock Shadow casts create a divided focus for the audience, giving them two things to look at, but it adds something special to the *Rocky* experience. At this point, it would be disappointing to attend a *Rocky Horror* screening without a shadow cast. It's now an expected part of the experience, just like props and shout-outs.

John Goldstone I've attended several midnight screenings over the years, which have been intense. The way that fans developed the shadow cast on top of the movie is so clever.

Jeffrey Weinstock The shadow cast phenomenon started in 1977 at the 8th Street Playhouse in New York—where the official Rocky Horror Fan Club was also born. From there, it spread out across the country. So the evolution of the cult following followed this trajectory: shout-outs, then costumes, then props, then shadow casts. It took a few months of *Rocky Horror* playing as a midnight movie before the callouts really started taking hold. But once they did, the audience participation just kept getting bigger—and it never stopped.

Sal Piro In spring of 1977, a young woman named Dori Hartley came to the Waverly to see *Rocky* for the first time. No one could guess at the profound effect she was to have on the development of the cult. The next Friday, she saw the film again. After that, she did not miss a showing of *Rocky* until the end of its run at the Waverly six months later. The more Dori saw the film, the more her obsession with Frank grew. At her thirteenth viewing, she appeared wearing makeup identical to Frank's and a cape like his that she made herself. Outside, the crowd waiting in line applauded her. She was encouraged by the response and worked constantly to improve her costume and makeup. It was Dori who reintroduced special clothing for the film, and it was here to stay.

Dori Hartley I will always remember that first walk I took as Frank, the day I dressed up for the first time. No one had done anything like that before, and I was lost in this buzzed-out Frank-trance. I could have walked into a car, right there in front of the Waverly, but somehow, I found myself, in full costume, walking alongside the line of people waiting to get tickets. Everyone's mouth dropped

Opposite: The legendary 8th Street Playhouse in New York City. Rocky Horror played there from July 21, 1978, until the theater closed in November 1992.
Left: Dori Hartley as Frank with Nell Campbell and Patricia Quinn.
Below: The original shadow cast Frank (Dori Hartley).

open, and they busted into this big applause. Holy moly, that was it. Nothing was ever the same, ever again. I went from regular ol' art student to Greenwich Village cult of personality! Getting famous for what I did wasn't part of the plan. I was simply a teenager who happened to have done something that nobody else did before me, so it caused a lot of attention. I've gone through life being known as "the first Frank." Who knew we'd make history? Not I. But I did know that from the very first time I flounced down that aisle at the Waverly, life would never again be the same.

Lillias Piro Dori Hartley came to *Rocky Horror* before me. She came with [my brother] Sal. I remember her. If you were in Dori Hartley's presence, you would not forget her. She was an incredible spirit. She was the right person at the right time to start putting on those costumes and become Frank. Dori took it to another level. She really embodied Tim Curry.

Sean Waters I was in ninth grade, and I was on the streets. I was a runaway and a survivor. I ran away from home. Because of *Rocky*, I was locked in a theater from 10 until 4 in the morning every Friday and Saturday night, whereas I could have been doing all sorts of shit. I performed as Riff Raff in the shadow cast, and I took it very seriously. The first time I put on his costume was life-changing. I felt like an instant celebrity. The Waverly Theater was bigger than any off-Broadway show in New York City. It sold out every single weekend, Friday, Saturday night. Waiting-lines-around-the-corner sold out. Being Riff was a big deal. And here I am, fifteen years old. Being in that theater kept me safe.

Susan Sarandon I remember taking Natalie Portman to a midnight screening when we were working on a movie together. She wanted to go, and—thank God—she didn't say it was her first time, because they would have torn her to pieces! They knew we were coming, and the people performing the shadow cast in front of the screen—playing out the movie as it happened—well, their parents had met doing that same thing. And now here they were, teenagers, carrying on the tradition.

Karen Tongson For the shadow cast, it's almost like a process of their own becoming. It's a chance to act out who they want to be,

Opposite: Shadow Brad and Janet now (top); and shadow Columbia, Frank, and Magenta then (bottom). Below: Shadow cast players in New York City.

who they wish they could be, or how they might express themselves freely if given the opportunity. That's not to say that every shadow cast member has a secret identity they need an outlet for, but it's about self-expression in a way that's liberating.

Sal Piro 20th Century Fox, the producer, saw that the shadow cast were good marketing tools. We were better than their paid people.

Barry Bostwick I was invited to the Tiffany Theater in LA a few years after the movie had become a hit. It was really interesting to see the audience-participation aspect of it. And the shadow cast called me up onstage and they presented me with a gold album. The show had just gone gold, and they gave me an album, framed and everything. I gave them a pair of framed tighty-whities in return. I'm one of the few actors in the world who can give away his underwear without being too creepy about it.

"I'll never forget the day Sal Piro handed me a bag of authentic costumes straight from the Belasco production. Definitely one of the best memories. Also, Sue Blane gave me Frank's original dinner shirt—whoa, that blew my mind! The dinner shirt, yes!"

—Dori Hartley

Trixie Mattel When I was shadow casting, they had this rule: Never look at the screen, because if the audience sees your eyes, they can tell you're looking at the screen and that you don't know it. But also, it's *Rocky Horror*. The audience and cast are drunk. It's not Cirque du Soleil.

Barry Bostwick The shadow casts all over the country, and the world, are there because they're exploring who they are, which would have been criticized for either their looks, their sexuality, or their ambivalence about their sexuality. When I've met these shadow casts, I'm always astonished about how this movie has made it okay for them to be just who they are, how they look, whatever their weight is, and whatever their sexuality is. I have become Uncle Barry to so many of these kids. And I love them all.

Sean Waters We didn't get paid for being in the shadow cast. We got free soda refills. But it was an honor to do it. *Rocky* shadow casts need to live on. They already have a life of their own. They will never go away. In America, they're in pretty much every city now.

Sue Blane To see it as a movie, *The Rocky Horror Picture Show*, acted out for real in the cinema by a shadow cast, I couldn't get my head around it. I still can't.

Opposite: Shadow Frank and Rocky have their shadowing down to a science (top); and Richard O'Brien with a shadow Frank (bottom).

With the shadow casts and audience-participation rituals up and running—and ever evolving— by summer 1977, Rocky Horror's transformation to the dark side was complete. Over the next decade, and well into the 1990s, and right up until today, Rocky, for many millions of young and queer people, is an indispensable part of growing up and feeling safe. The cult was born.

Richard O'Brien I had a moment when I realized *Rocky* was gaining cult status. We were in Florida not long after the movie opened, and my son Linus, who was very young, was playing in the pool at a Holiday Inn. As we left, I called him from the pool, and an American couple overheard. The woman said under her breath, "That's Riff Raff" as I turned away. I wasn't sure if she was being rude or referencing the character. It was a little moment, but telling.

Sal Piro It's great that a new generation seems to find it every year or two, and it's fun to see the virgins [viewers seeing it for the first time]. They don't want to be as hostile to the performers as the veterans. Some of them love it, and some are so stunned they never come back. They're a good mix with the veterans, the 100- and 150-timers. New York audiences tend to be more sophisticated with the lines. Sometimes in the suburbs, when the floor show comes on, you'll hear some idiot yelling, "Hey, faggot!" But management takes care of it. They make a lot of money from the candy we buy.

John Goldstone It's so interesting that it was a failure on release and then found a fandom in a big way, which has been continuous and loyal for fifty years. It obviously has something going for it!

Jeffrey Weinstock The early *Rocky Horror* audience was overwhelmingly young and significantly queer. A large percentage of those early fans were from the LGBT community or otherwise felt alienated from mainstream society.

Sue Blane It was picked up in New York and turned into a cult film. So, it's thanks to the fans in New York that we've had a living out of work, frankly.

Trixie Mattel I remember reading a copy of the Guinness Book of World Records in elementary school and seeing a picture from *Rocky Horror*. It showed what I thought was a waitress—Magenta—in fishnets. Next to her was someone dressed as Frank-N-Furter. I didn't know what I was looking at back then, but even then, I was blown away. People went to a movie dressed up in costume? I didn't know when else you'd see that, except when a movie becomes part of a big cultural phenomenon.

Jack Black *Rocky Horror* was bigger than its story—it was bigger than a movie. Watching it felt like being part of a movement, something that connected with us on a deep level, making us feel accepted, loved, and celebrated.

Sean Waters *Rocky* was a home for a lot of wayward souls, the misfits, people that were eccentric, people that didn't always fit in. When I went to my first screening at the Waverly, I found my tribe. I found people, and I belonged to some place—and I was a runaway, so I needed to belong. And I belonged. At first, I didn't go nuts. But by end of the movie, I was like, "I'll be here tomorrow night!" And I religiously went for years.

Jim Sharman I'd love to say we foresaw everything that *Rocky Horror* would become. We didn't. We were just trying to put on a great show. Everything that followed—the cult, the midnight screenings, the phenomenon—that's something you can't create deliberately. It happens organically, decided by forces outside of you.

"As 1977 was ending, we were on top of the world and having the time of our lives. In our wildest imaginations, though, we never dreamed of the dramatic future lying ahead for the cult of *Rocky* audience participation. Already the media—newspapers, magazines, you name it—had begun to pick up on what was going on at the Waverly."

—Sal Piro

EPILOGUE

With one final, perverted pelvic thrust and a jump to the left, we find ourselves at the end. But wait, before Magenta's luscious red lips kiss us all goodbye (for now), there's a happy ending to be had. *Rocky Horror*'s legacy lingers in the air, forever on the hunt for fresh souls to feast upon with every new generation. It is a titan, an icon of popular culture, and a bright beacon of hope for misfits, outcasts, the queer—and, don't forget, the regular Joes—all of whom really found *Rocky* quite pleasurable time after time. Before we leave, there's only one more thing to add: Another slice, anyone?

You don't need us to tell you how important The Rocky Horror Show, *and its endless stream of associated multimedia and merchandise, has become over the years. And we won't. We'll leave that to its creators, cast, crew, collaborators, and coconspirators, of all whom contribute to* Rocky Horror *keeping its legendary status.*

Richard O'Brien *Rocky* was a piece of adolescent fun. A boys' bedroom musical. It has nothing of great import to say. It's not a political piece. It's just what it is: a piece of nonsense. It's very entertaining, and it's not a bad yarn. As a piece of storytelling and entertainment, it's perfectly good and enjoyable and fun. But for it to have had this longevity . . . it doesn't make a great deal of sense.

Jim Sharman *Rocky* has become the longest-running film of all time. It's a phenomenon that eludes commercial logic, but there must be something in the DNA of the movie. The fans made it a phenomenon.

Jeffrey Weinstock In 2005, *Rocky Horror* was added to the Library of Congress as a historically significant film. Think about that. It debuted as a flop and was pulled from distribution in less than two months. Now, it's officially recognized as a culturally important work. That's a huge shift in perception.

Richard O'Brien One reason for *Rocky Horror's* lasting impact is that it's a fairy tale, a parable, an allegory. Parables and allegories are often more effective than overt messages. Its roots in stories like Genesis, "Hansel and Gretel," and the babes in the wood make it universally accessible. These stories are familiar, and *Rocky* taps into that, offering a rite-of-passage story. Instead of a gingerbread house, we have Frankenstein Place, and instead of the Wicked Witch, we have Frank-N-Furter as the evil force in the protagonists' lives.

I think the kids are also responding to *Rocky* because there's an element of naivete about it which is very endearing and not threatening. Its innocence is its strength. All the characters appear to be sophisticated, knowledgeable people, but they're really not. That allows people of a similar adolescent nature to feel they could be part of the whole thing. And now, in fact, they are.

"*Rocky* is now fifty years old. It was only meant to run for three weeks."

—Richard O'Brien

Trixie Mattel At this point in history, specifically American history, you would hope *Rocky Horror* would be a relic—a part of the past. "People used to be afraid of a woman in a suit or a man in a dress, or someone expressing a gender identity somewhere between two genders." I wish we lived in a world where we could explain that this used to be a problem, but we don't.

Lillias Piro Everything to do with *Rocky* was fresh, new, innovative. Even in 1977, I'd never seen a man in fishnets or a corset. There was an electricity about *Rocky Horror* that no one could understand unless you were there.

Tristan Ratterman The thing that sets *Rocky Horror* apart from every other movie musical, I would argue, is it hits an interest for everybody. You know, it hits the rock and roll. It hits the nostalgic vintage appeal that's really popular right now. It hits the science fiction, the horror, the musical—I mean, everything. There's something in it for absolutely everybody.

Karen Tongson There are so many things about *Rocky* that give it lasting power, but I think, fundamentally, what sustains its power is the audience. The way it inspired and triggered something in groups of people that has endured through generations. These traditions—the shadow casts, the interactive screenings, the midnight showings across five decades—are what make it truly unique. It's about the film exceeding its own boundaries and becoming a cultural phenomenon that has changed people's lives. That's why it's important. That's why its legacy continues to be honored today.

Trixie Mattel The enthusiasm for *Rocky* is unmatched. I don't know what it is, but people go regularly, dress up, and throw things. People have kept going for decades. Just a couple of weeks ago, I went to a *Rocky* screening, and the person who hired me when I started working with *Rocky* was sitting next to me—this person had been

BARRY BOSTWICK
Show - Megaforce - Spin City
DAMMIT JANET I love You!

there with me when I was eighteen, and now they were sitting there with their teenage kids. I thought, wow! It's amazing how it spans generations.

Joel Thurm Tim Curry should have been knighted by now, surely?

Jeffrey Weinstock There are different types of cult films. There's the so-bad-it's-good cult film—*The Room* obviously falls into that category. Then there's just the weird and the strange as another type of cult film. Sometimes people talk about passionate allegiance to major-release films—like the cult of *The Princess Bride*, or people who dress up as *Star Wars* characters—but they don't tend to think of those as cult films. To my mind, a cult film is *Rocky*.

What gives *Rocky Horror* its lasting power is the sheer enjoyment at its core. I think it was made to be fun. It was made to be enjoyed. In some ways, it was made for people to participate in its spirit—even if the creators didn't anticipate that people would actually get up out of their seats and shout at the screen.

Trixie Mattel I sit down and watch *Rocky Horror* every Halloween, and honestly, every October, I reflect on it. I wouldn't have anything I have now—my career, my sense of security with myself—if it weren't for the "homosexual water aerobics" of doing *Rocky*.

Jeffrey Weinstock Once upon a time, *Rocky Horror* was outsider entertainment—something you went to if you wanted to be a little edgy. Today, it's almost a rite of passage. It's become the thing that high school or college kids do at least once.

Barry Bostwick After the movie was made, and when I started becoming aware of its popularity ten years later, I started doing interviews and conventions. Thanks to *Rocky*, it has been a huge part of my life to associate with so many different groups of people in this world and in the world of show business.

"*West Side Story*, *Guys and Dolls*, and *My Fair Lady* are the three greatest musicals ever written. If *Rocky* is somewhere near the top ten, I would be perfectly happy."

—Richard O'Brien

Richard O'Brien They've asked a lot of people to interpret the show's success, and they all seem to miss the very obvious answer: It allows the kids to dress up. I see guys on the street in fishnet stockings and corsets, and I think it's terrific. It's a major breakthrough. Women have been cross-dressing for years. Now they can wear almost anything, but a man can't. Thanks to *Rocky Horror*, a guy can put on fishnets and strut his stuff and feel okay. I see no harm in that at all.

Jack Black Watching *Rocky Horror* at age nine had a major effect on me. There are a few key events in my childhood and teenage years that changed the course of my life, and *Rocky Horror* was one of them. The combination of rock and roll music and audience participation really ignited something in me, and it was a big reason why I followed my path into music and acting. I love that mix of rock and theater. I started Tenacious D with Kyle [Gass], and we incorporate a lot of theatricality into our shows. We definitely owe a debt of gratitude to *Rocky Horror*.

John Goldstone *Rocky Horror* could never be made now, but that's okay. The original film will live forever.

Barry Bostwick gets a visit from a fan at the Motor City Comic Con, 2025.

Richard with Peter Blake, who took over the role of Frank in the London production, c. 1978.

Ford

Lillias Piro I wasn't alive until I saw *The Rocky Horror Picture Show*. I walked through life. I was unhappy. I certainly wasn't getting any dates. I was miserable. I went from that to watching that screen, wanting to be who I wanted to be, and I was fabulous.

Karen Tongso Some people go to church every Sunday to sing the same songs over and over again to feel free and hopeful. The people who go to *Rocky Horror* every week do the same thing: They go to their "church" to sing the songs, to find comfort for their souls, and to experience freedom and hope. The ritual of going every week is part of that experience.

Jack Black Isn't it funny that *Rocky Horror* as a concept—both the play and the movie—came out of the '60s, the sexual revolution, and a new freedom of expression? It was all about being who we are and living without fear of judgment or violence. And here we are, fifty years later, still dealing with the same issues. It's crazy, but it just shows you that the power of *Rocky Horror* is still as relevant and necessary as ever.

Jim Sharman I'm sure many have tried to replicate what *Rocky Horror*—both the film and the show—achieved, but it has never quite happened. That's because it was created sincerely, with a great deal of love. Everyone involved grew up loving late-night movies, and they ended up making the ultimate late-night movie.

Lou Adler Like many people who got involved with *Rocky Horror*, those who truly understood what it was about were few. Richard O'Brien, Sue Blane, and Tim—those were the ones who really got it. They were unique in the best way, and I think if anyone else had been involved, *Rocky Horror* wouldn't have been what it became. The audience that kept coming back understood that uniqueness too.

Jack Black Any movie with rock music owes a debt to *Rocky Horror*. *School of Rock*, *Spinal Tap*, and *Little Shop of Horrors* all tip their hats to it, because it was the first to really bring rock and roll to the big screen.

Lillias Piro (left) doing "The Time Warp" with Patricia Quinn at an anniversary showing of the movie.

Dori Hartley *Rocky Horror* was more than a phenomenon—it was a phenomenon that was a product of the times, which were the '70s. In the '70s, this was breakout thinking. Now, *Rocky Horror* is sweet, even naive. *Rocky Horror*'s appeal is both daring and wholesome.

Trixie Mattel *Rocky* is the beginning of queerness in America. You could go to a screening, put on a bra and panties as a man, and you're participating in American culture. It doesn't say anything about your gender or sexuality; it actually makes you cool. It's about rolling with it and being part of something bigger.

Belinda Sinclair *Rocky Horror* was more than a musical; it was alive. It was funny but also tragic at times. One moment you were in love with Frank-N-Furter, and the next, you felt sorry for him. You laughed at Brad and Janet, but then you felt scared for them. There was so much emotional depth.

Richard O'Brien and Richard Hartley during the filming of Strange Journey.

Susan Sarandon I wouldn't mind at all if *Rocky* was my legacy. I am so proud to have been part of *The Rocky Horror Picture Show* and to be part of that group and phenomenon. The message that keeps going out—"Don't dream it, be it"—is just so pure, optimistic, and perfect. It encourages people to find their authentic self and do it with love. That's a beautiful thing to be a part of.

Tim Curry I'm very proud of the film because it's had such an effect over many years. I don't know if being Frank is really any great achievement, but I am proud of it.

Richard O'Brien *The Rocky Horror Show* has opened a lot of doors for me. It cemented friendships. It has given me a lot of pleasure. Despite my so-called success, I guess I still see myself as an actor who is temporarily unemployed.

Richard Hartley I feel proud of the show. We did what we thought worked best for that moment in the show. We didn't overthink it. We worked things out quickly. If the show and movie have had a positive impact on people's lives, you can't really ask for more than that. That doesn't happen to every musical.

Peter Hinwood I've just been proud of my role and the cult following. People send me photos from America asking for autographs, which is strange. I didn't feel like I achieved much, but now it seems like something I'll be remembered for. When I die, I suppose it'll say something about *Rocky Horror* on my gravestone.

Jim Sharman At this point, maybe it deserves a special Oscar for longevity?

In spring 1977, superfan Sal Piro created the official Rocky Horror Picture Show Fan Club and remained president until his death in 2023. The club, with its newsletter, became a way for fans to communicate, share information about screenings, and pass along new audience traditions and rituals. It was also a safe place where* Rocky *fans could find like-minded friends—and themselves.

LIMITED EDITION

278

VOL. 2 NO. 4

FLASH R.H.P.S.

IT WAS A NIGHT OUT WE WERE GOING TO REMEMBER FOR A VERY LONG TIME

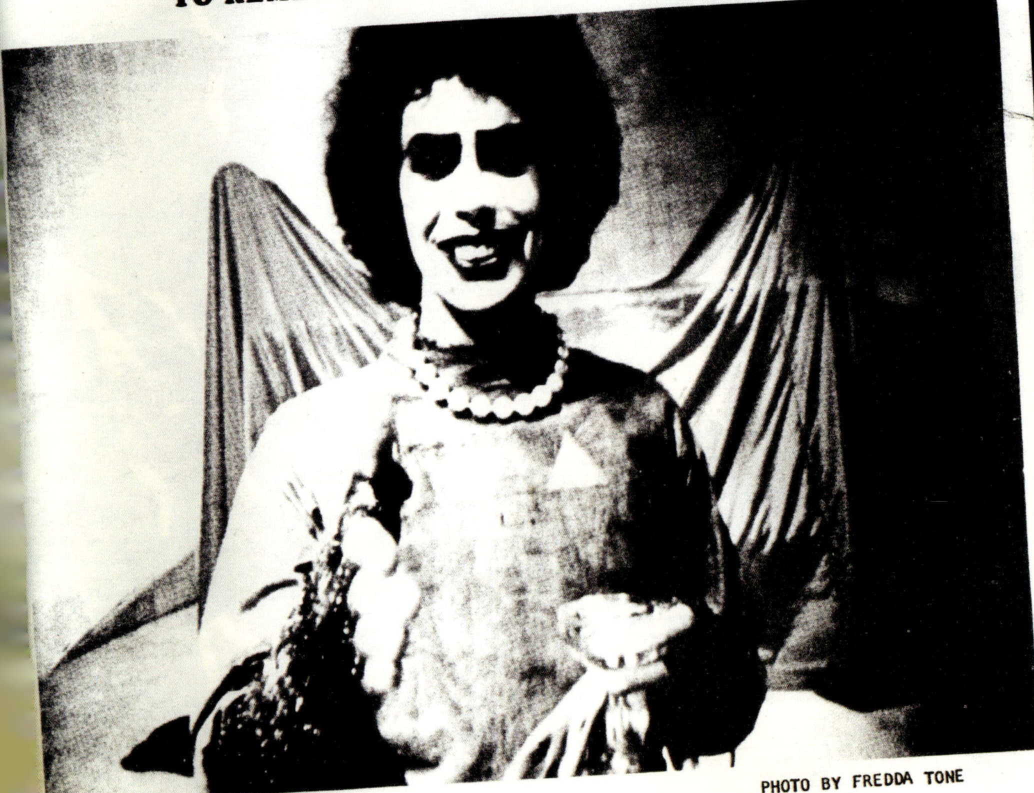

PHOTO BY FREDDA TONE

A SPECIAL ISSUE FANZINE FOR THE ROCKY HORROR FAN CLUB

RROR PICTURE SHOW
N CLUB
reet, New York City, NY 10011

HORROR NEWS
ANNIVERSARY EDITION

on the board game) with Madeline
December release...The previous
n Curry's film LEGEND has been
ce response in European previews,
be released...Susan Sarandon has
h of a baby girl, her new film
cal and box office success...
successful run in the play
ic Theater...Meanwhile, in London,
a Shakespearean play with the
CKY HORROR 10th Anniversary
special on USA Cable's NIGHT
hard O'Brien will host USA
nd 5...The ROCKY HORROR PICTURE
subject of articles and reports
USA TODAY, and hundreds of local
newspapers and local radio shows...in New York City Fan Club President Sal Piro was the guest on the Jay Thomas show on K-Rock radio. K-Rock is the official station of the anniversary and has given away 100 tickets to the event....Following the success of the anniversary look for the release of new ROCKY HORROR products including the ROCKY HORROR make-up kit and a new line of ROCKY HORROR buttons. For future merchandise information send a s.a.s.e. (business size) to the fan club and specify merchandise information...Also a video game has been released in Europe based on THE ROCKY HORROR SHOW. There is a possibility it will be brought to the United States by Activision...

LET'S DO THE TIME WARP AGAIN!!

Horrors!

THE film's been out 10 years and made $60 million, but the South African government has just discovered *The Rocky Horror Show* — and banned it. The Pretoria folks had thought it was just another American sci-fi flick until someone decided to screen it and found out the main character is a transvestite vampire. Despite that blow, everyone connected with the movie will be gathering Halloween night at the Beacon Theater on upper Broadway to celebrate the film's 10th anniversary with producers Lou Adler and, in from England, Michael White. Barry Bostwick and Susan Sarandon are also expected and Tim Curry, rehearsing in London with the Royal Shakespeare Co., is going to try to fly in as well.

★ ★ ★

BROOMSTICKS: Richard O'Brien, Little Nell, Jonathan Adams and other stars from *The Rocky Horror Picture Show* will show up at the Beacon Theater on Halloween to celebrate the movie's 10th anniversary.

The dark-humored cult film has taken in more than $60 million at the box office, mostly from midnight showings.

LET'S DO THE TIME WARP AGAIN!!

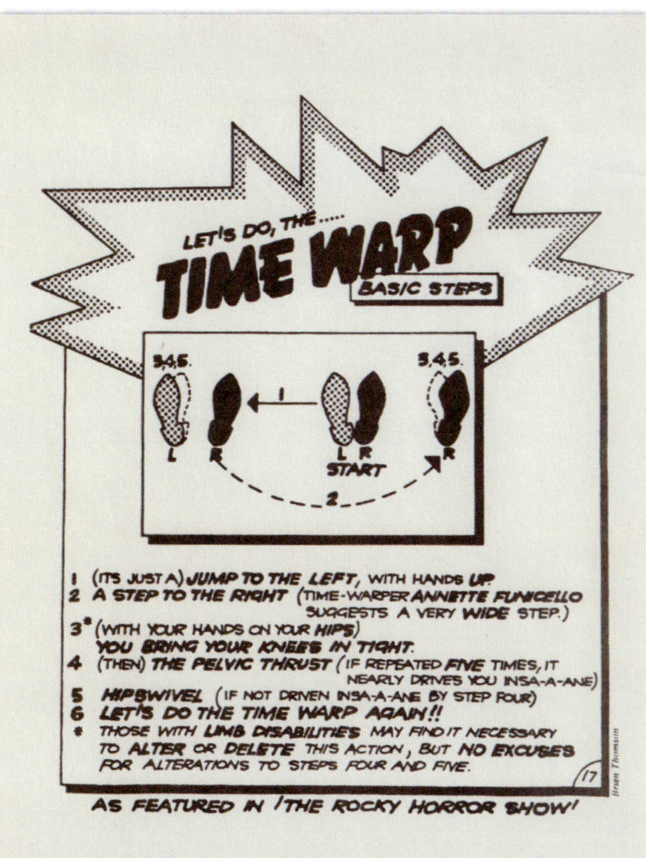
LET'S DO, THE.....

TIME WARP

BASIC STEPS

3,4,5. 3,4,5.

L R 1 L R START R

2

1 (ITS JUST A) JUMP TO THE LEFT, WITH HANDS UP

2 A STEP TO THE RIGHT (TIME-WARPER ANNETTE FUNICELLO SUGGESTS A VERY WIDE STEP.)

3* (WITH YOUR HANDS ON YOUR HIPS) YOU BRING YOUR KNEES IN TIGHT.

4 (THEN) THE PELVIC THRUST (IF REPEATED FIVE TIMES, IT NEARLY DRIVES YOU INSA-A-ANE)

5 HIPSWIVEL (IF NOT DRIVEN INSA-A-ANE BY STEP FOUR)

6 LET'S DO THE TIME WARP AGAIN!!

* THOSE WITH LIMB DISABILITIES MAY FIND IT NECESSARY TO ALTER OR DELETE THIS ACTION, BUT NO EXCUSES FOR ALTERATIONS TO STEPS FOUR AND FIVE.

17

Brian Thomson

AS FEATURED IN 'THE ROCKY HORROR SHOW'

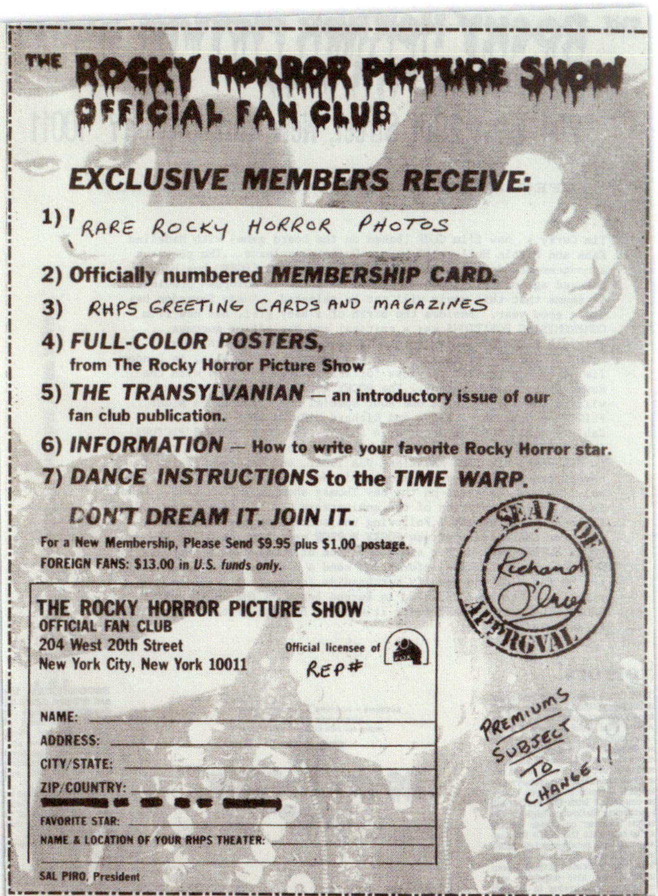
THE ROCKY HORROR PICTURE SHOW

OFFICIAL FAN CLUB

EXCLUSIVE MEMBERS RECEIVE:

1) RARE ROCKY HORROR PHOTOS

2) Officially numbered MEMBERSHIP CARD.

3) RHPS GREETING CARDS AND MAGAZINES

4) FULL-COLOR POSTERS, from The Rocky Horror Picture Show

5) THE TRANSYLVANIAN — an introductory issue of our fan club publication.

6) INFORMATION — How to write your favorite Rocky Horror star.

7) DANCE INSTRUCTIONS to the TIME WARP.

DON'T DREAM IT. JOIN IT.

For a New Membership, Please Send $9.95 plus $1.00 postage.
FOREIGN FANS: $13.00 in U.S. funds only.

SEAL OF APPROVAL — Richard O'Brien

THE ROCKY HORROR PICTURE SHOW
OFFICIAL FAN CLUB
204 West 20th Street
New York City, New York 10011

Official licensee of
REP#

PREMIUMS SUBJECT TO CHANGE!!

NAME:
ADDRESS:
CITY/STATE:
ZIP/COUNTRY:
FAVORITE STAR:
NAME & LOCATION OF YOUR RHPS THEATER:

SAL PIRO, President

Opposite: One of the original fanzines for the Rocky Horror Fan Club.
Above: President of the Rocky Horror Fan Club, Sal Piro.

Jeffrey Weinstock Sal Piro was already a *Rocky Horror* elder, an MC at the 8th Street Playhouse, and a coordinator of the shadow cast—sometimes even performing himself. Like so many others, he became completely obsessed with the film, but he took it a step further—organizing a fan club, helping establish the shadow cast tradition, and cowriting *The Transylvanian* newsletter with his sister. The club helped spread the idea of shadow casting to other cities. He became the face of *Rocky Horror* fandom.

Lillias Piro I first heard about *Rocky* in 1976 when my brother Sal came home to our home in Jersey City. I was twelve years old. We were very close. He had to share everything with me. He said, "I saw this amazing film." He was so animated and so passionate about it. And then he said to me, "Don't worry, I'll take you." He did. It was March of 1977, at the Waverly in the Village. The audience participation was already starting to take shape. I sat down in the middle of the fifth row and watched Sal give his now-legendary announcements.

A lot of people know Sal as the president of the Rocky Horror Fan Club until he died. He started the club in a little apartment on West Fourth Street. He ran the club because *Rocky* started taking off all over the country, and people were writing to the club like Sal was Santa Claus with big bags of mail. It got to the point where Sal had to employ people to help him answer fans' questions. There are people out there to this day that will still contact me and tell me, "I have a letter from your brother that he wrote me personally."

Above: Frank and Magenta preparing for Rocky's birth—and the birth of a phenomenon.
Opposite: The poster for the release of the movie in Japan.

While once described by its own father, Richard O'Brien, as nothing more than "silly nonsense," the truth is that Rocky *is hugely important—essential—to millions of people as an icon of liberation and self-expression. Underneath all the makeup and corsets lies a vital philosophy of hope and inclusivity for the LGBTQIA+ community, of which* Rocky Horror *will forever be a powerful ally.*

Richard O'Brien Until very recently, I've argued that *Rocky* is just a piece of silly nonsense. But the religious right in America have started becoming vocal and horrible. Nationalism is terrifying. The lack of kindness towards the LGBT+ community is astonishing. And we're taking steps backward. So I think maybe *Rocky* is becoming more important by default. *Rocky* is a place for the marginalized. I see *Rocky* now as a rainbow event. I'm not a flag waver. But the flag I would stand by is the rainbow flag. And I think *Rocky* is important in that respect.

Nell Campbell So many people have told me they were suicidal until they found *Rocky*. Richard has always described himself as being at war with himself. And the people who have embraced *Rocky* have felt that way too—and they, too, felt released by the show. Without doubt the greatest aspect of the film. And for me being part of it, that it has had such a moving, extraordinary effect and helped so many.

Jim Sharman The message on stage and screen was always a sense of liberation. That was at the heart of it all.

Lillias Piro *Rocky Horror* has remained relevant in the '70s, '90s, aughties, and now. We need *Rocky Horror* more than eve, because we need to let children be who they are today. Today's culture in the US is going backward in regard to gender and sexuality. What Richard wrote fifty years ago would be wasted if we now go backward. We need to allow children, people, to be who they want to be. That's how the world stays interesting. That's how the world stays fabulous. That's how the world goes round.

Karen Tongson *Rocky Horror* invites us to imagine, no matter who we are or what our identities are, what it would be like if we let ourselves become who we wanted to be. For women, the character of

THE ROCKY HORROR PICTURE SHOW

[ロッキー・ホラー・ショー]

He's the hero–
that's right,
the hero!!

ティム・カリー
スーザン・サランドン
バリー・ボストウィック
リチャード・オブライエン
パトリシア・クイン
リトル・ネル
ジョナサン・アダムス
ピーター・ハインウッド
ミートローフ
チャールズ・グレイ

製作総指揮■ルー・アドラー
製作■マイケル・ホワイト
監督■ジム・シャーマン
原作ミュージカル作詞+作曲■リチャード・オブライエン
脚本■ジム・シャーマン
リチャード・オブライエン
音楽監督+編曲■リチャード・ハートレイ

1975年 アメリカ映画 カラー 99分
配給=ユーロスペース+シネマライズ・渋谷
協賛=日本たばこ産業株式会社

20th CENTURY FOX

THE ROCKY HORROR PICTURE SHOW
THE LOU ADLER / MICHAEL WHITE PRODUCTION FOR 20TH CENTURY FOX

Above: No matter who you are during the day, everyone can be a sweet transvestite at midnight.
Opposite: Our hero—that's right, our hero!

Janet and her sexual liberation—it's queer, in the sense that she's attracted to a range of people. What makes *Rocky Horror* unique for the LGBTQ+ community is that it wasn't just a film to access. It was a life experience—where we could find people who were like us or at least people who also felt like outsiders.

Lillias Piro *Rocky Horror* had a significant part in opening the minds and the hearts of people who wanted to break all the rules. There was deep meaning to it, even if Richard O'Brien didn't even know what he was doing when he did it.

Belinda Sinclair We broke a lot of boundaries with the LGBTQ community. *Rocky* took it to the audience, showed them what it was, and said, "This is what it is. What are you going to do about it?"

Richard Hartley *Rocky* helped a lot of people. It was a place where people, no matter their gender or identity, could dress up, express themselves, and not be demonized for it.

Nell Campbell One of the reasons I think *Rocky Horror* is so divine is because it has an innocence to it. Everything feels natural. You don't choose your sexuality or the color of your skin. These things are celebrated in the show, as they should be, and they helped people who were ashamed of their sexual preferences—whether it was how they liked to dress or just being inhibited—not feel ashamed anymore.

John Goldstone While we were making the movie, we had no idea about its importance for the LGBTQ community. It was just a highly original work of entertainment that clearly worked well in the theater and could be made to work in the cinema. It's so extraordinary how what it evolved into was nothing that I expected. That people have discovered their sexuality through *Rocky* and been able to come out and realize who they are is possibly the movie's greatest achievement.

Richard O'Brien The element of transvestism wasn't intended as a major theme, although it turned out to be one. Writing a transvestite into the play was a very naive judgment. Maybe there was a lot of subconscious feeling about that subject coming through. I don't know. I've always thought of Frank as a cross between Ivan the Terrible and Cruella de Vil of Walt Disney's *One Hundred and One Dalmatians*.

Opposite: Nell Campbell during the original London production. Above: Patricia Quinn and Richard O'Brien in the movie. Following page: Richard in front of the Riff Raff statue at the Waikato Museum in New Zealand.

Patricia Quinn As far as I'm concerned, we were doing sex, drugs, and rock and roll. That was our show. Then it became this amazing liberation movement, which I understand now—but at the time, I didn't really connect with it that way. For me, it was just an incredibly entertaining piece of work. We weren't setting out to change the world. We were just making Frankenstein—again.

Nell Campbell People often ask me why *The Rocky Horror Picture Show* has lasted so triumphantly. I tell them: the play. It was ninety minutes with no interval, witty, original, and incredibly sexy. I can't think of many other musicals that are sexy. I didn't even find *Hair* sexy. The fact that it embraces all kinds of sexuality and has meant so much to the LGBTQ community certainly helps. It is a celebration of all things heterosexual, homosexual, transsexual, bisexual, cross-dressing, you name it—it's a celebration of all of them.

Barry Bostwick The movie, and how it has encouraged people to explore their authentic selves, has actually affected me personally. I've seen a whole side of humanity that I would normally not have experienced if it wasn't for this movie. My experience with *The Rocky Horror Picture Show* has allowed me to trust finally my own thoughts, my own words, my own mind, and my own person in a public way. Actors have a tendency to hide behind characters, and *The Rocky Horror Picture Show* made me come out from behind the curtain as a human being.

Tim Curry Several people have told me that the movie, and the play, helped them to understand their sexuality, which I'm glad about. I think that's important.

John Goldstone The film has a really good message. "Don't dream it, be it" is a very important message that doesn't have to apply to just sexuality, but just generally a positive attitude to life. And the kids need to hear that. There are too many depressive attitudes for kids growing up and dealing with the realities of life when, in fact, "Don't dream it, be it" is a clear message of letting them be whoever they want to be.

Susan Sarandon "Don't dream it, be it"—that philosophy has liberated so many people, not just in terms of accepting their sexuality or gender identity, but in a broader sense. It's about getting out there and doing it. Don't dream it, be it.

o Museum
NGA O WAIKATO
CAUTION

“I remember a shadow cast performer saying to me, ‘It doesn’t matter what you think about *Rocky Horror* anymore, Richard. Because it’s not yours. It belongs to us, not to you.’ And I thought, ‘That’s absolutely true.’ ”

—Richard O’Brien

Acknowledgments

There were many people who went on the strange journey with me, to bring the documentary and these books to life. My thanks to go, Adam Gibbs, Garret Price, Avner Shiloah, Warren Kommers, Ben Kaufman, Loe Fahie, Nolan Peacock, Fenton Bailey, Nasim Mirkiani, Andy Leighton, Dixon Knox, Addie Poris, and Swampy Marsh.

At Weldon Owen, my thanks to editor Karyn Gerhard, publisher Roger Shaw, and assistant Jon Ellis for bringing this all together.

My eternal gratitude to all of the people who shared their stories for the documentary, making the text of this book possible: Jim Sharman, Lou Adler, Tim Curry, Susan Sarandon, Barry Bostwick, Patricia Quinn, Nell Campbell, Peter Hinwood, Chrissie Messenger, Belinda Sinclair, Sue Blane, John Goldstone, Jack Black, and Trixie Mattel.

And finally, to my family—Dad, Mom, Elvis O'Brien, Sabrina Graf, Josh O'Brien, Kim O'Brien, Boosh, Lai Lai, Gart, Amelia Walters, Joe Walters, Thea Walters, and Finn Walters—without whose love and support none of this would have been possible.

—Linus

Interview and Photo Credits

Archival Interviews

Rayner Bourton
Rayner Bourton Convention Q&A, UK Transylvania Rocky Horror Convention, 1999.

Tim Deegan
"After a poor box office showing in Los Angeles, . . ." "50 Years of Rocky Horror Picture Show" by Jada Shavers, December 2, 2022.

Dori Hartley
Interview by Sal Piro, Rockyhorror.com, December 6, 2011.

Meat Loaf
"My background with theatre . . ." Interview by Ken Sharp, *Goldmine Magazine*, January 21, 2022.
"Richard and Jim came to me for the part of 'Hot Patootie,' . . ." "VH1 Behind the Music," written and produced by Jason Goodman, 1999.
"Elvis Presley came to see the stage version . . ." "Meat Loaf the singer was also a Hollywood actor: His most noteworthy movie roles revealed," Stephanie Nolasco, Fox 13, January 21, 2022.
"I went to a sold-out midnight screening . . ." Meat Loaf interview on the *Late Show with David Letterman*, August 12, 1982.

Sal Piro
Creatures of the Night: The Rocky Horror Experience, Stabur Corporation, October 1, 1990.

Brian Thomson
"Exclusive Interview: A Conversation with the Big Banana of Anti-set Design in *Rocky Horror*." Interview by Patricia Morrisoe, RockyMusic.org, 1979.

Photos

All images courtesy the Richard O'Brien estate, except where noted below:

T=Top, B=Bottom, L=Left, R=Right, C=Center

Alamy Stock House: 120–21, 165, *Alain Le Garsmeur* 110T, *Allstar Picture Library Ltd* 148–49, *Everett Collection Inc,* 110B, *Photo 12* 160, 164T, *Pictorial Press Ltd* 46, 110C, *TCD/Prod.DB* 164BR, 177, *20th Century Fox* 202; **Courtesy the Brian Weinberg Estate:** 186T, 186B, 197T, 197B; **© Douglas H. Jeffery / Victoria and Albert Museum, London** 61, 72–73, 82, 89; **Everett Collection:** 115, 124, 176. © *Joe Gaffney* 87, *Mary Evans / Ronald Grant* 151, *Mary Evans / © 20TH CENTURY FOX / Ronald Grant* 147, 215, *Priscilla Grant* 204, © *20th Century Fox Film Corp.* 112L, 150, 154–55, 170, 172BR, 173, 212, 213; **Getty Images:** *Bromberger Hoover Photography* 198, *Dave M. Benett* 129, *Evening Standard / Stringer* 52, 65, 100, *Movie Poster Image Art* 136-37, *Michael Ochs Archives* 116, *Michael Ochs Archives / Stringer* 101, *Mirrorpix* 25, *Santiago Felipe* 10, *Stanley Bielecki Movie Collection* 112R, 134B, 139, 159, *WWD* 104; **© Interfishnet Ltd.**: 92–93; **© John Jay / mptvimages.com:** 2, 16–17, 105, 123, 125, 126, 127, 128, 131, 132–33, 134T, 135 all, 136–37, 138, 142, 143, 144–45, 152, 153, 158, 163, 164BL, 166, 167 all, 168, 172T, 200, 223; **Kimi Wong:** 31, 32, 47, 49, 64, 67 all, 220, 221; **Mark Jabara:** 57, 58, 60, 76, 84, 85, 90–91, 98–99, 102T, 106, 107–08, 174–75, 195, 211R, 198B; **mptvimages.com:** 128; **Photofest**: 217; **Photostage:** 4, 18–19, 56, 69, 78–79, 95, 111.

weldon**owen**

an imprint of Insight Editions
P.O. Box 3088
San Rafael, CA 94912
www.weldonowen.com

CEO Raoul Goff
SVP Group Publisher Jeff McLaughlin
VP Publisher Roger Shaw
Executive Editor Karyn Gerhard
Editorial Assistant Jon Ellis
Managing Editor Michelle Hope
VP Creative Chrissy Kwasnik
Art Director Megan Sinead Bingham
VP Manufacturing Alix Nicholaeff
Production Manager Joshua Smith
Strategic Production Planner Lina s Palma-Temena

Weldon Owen would also like to thank Sheri Linden and Lee Stokes.

Special thanks to Richard and Linus O'Brien, Charlie Day, Rebeckah Dalton, Malcolm Croft, and Roger Gorman; without their enthusiasm, talent, and spirit of collaboration, this book could not have been made. Our gratitude also goes to Mark Jabara, whose knowledge, generosity, and extensive archive was invaluable in the making of this book.

Design by Roger Gorman, Reiner Design Consultants, Inc.

ISBN: 979-8-88674-335-7

Manufactured in China by Insight Editions
10 9 8 7 6 5 4 3 2 1

REPLANTED PAPER